MW01629029

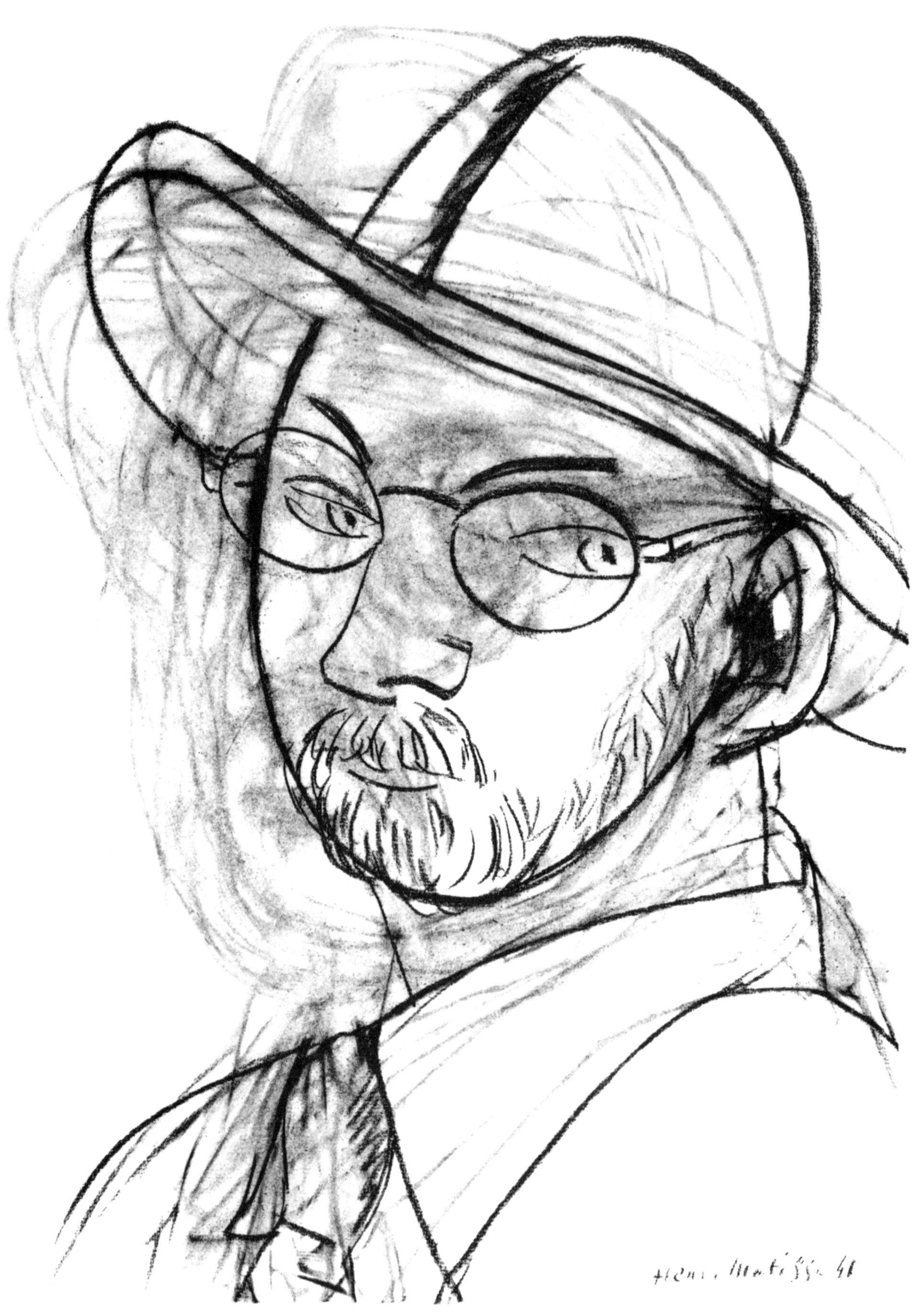

Self-portrait in a straw hat, 1941. Sanguine, 48 × 37 mm.

MATISSE
Portrait Drawings
45 Plates

by HENRI MATISSE

Dover Publications, Inc., New York

Publisher's Note

The portrait drawings of Henri Matisse (1869–1954) are marked by a facility of line and composition that gives no hint of the effort or concentration that went into them. Matisse said that he began to develop his portrait technique when, as a student, he was doodling as he waited in a post office. Giving his hand a free rein, he was amazed to see the likeness of his mother take shape on the paper. He realized that this lively portrait had been executed in a manner that was held to ridicule by the academicians with whom he studied (William-Adolphe Bouguereau being among their number), and that it was emotion and memory that allowed him to draw the image without recourse to a living model. As a result, he put great importance on the impression created by his first contact with the subject. In the initial sitting, Matisse would try to capture the essence of the model. He would wait a few days before doing further studies, evaluating his work in his mind, thinking of more technical and formal aspects. In the following sessions, the relation between artist and subject would be consolidated. Matisse said that he focused on the asymmetry of features that makes faces unique, following what he thought of as an approach of the Northern School as demonstrated by such masters as Hans Holbein the Younger, Albrecht Dürer and Lucas Cranach. And, while Matisse may not show a literal truth, the artist's firm contour line always reflects his deep knowledge of anatomy.

Matisse Portrait Drawings: 45 Plates is a new work, first published by Dover Publications, Inc., in 1990.

Manufactured in the United States of America
Dover Publications, Inc.
31 East 2nd Street
Mineola, N.Y. 11501

Library of Congress Cataloging-in-Publication Data

Matisse, Henri, 1869–1954.
Matisse portrait drawings / by Henri Matisse.
p. cm. — (Dover art library)
ISBN 0-486-26438-6
1. Matisse, Henri, 1869–1954—Catalogs. I. Title. II. Series.
NC248.M4A4 1990
714.944—dc20 90-37671
CIP

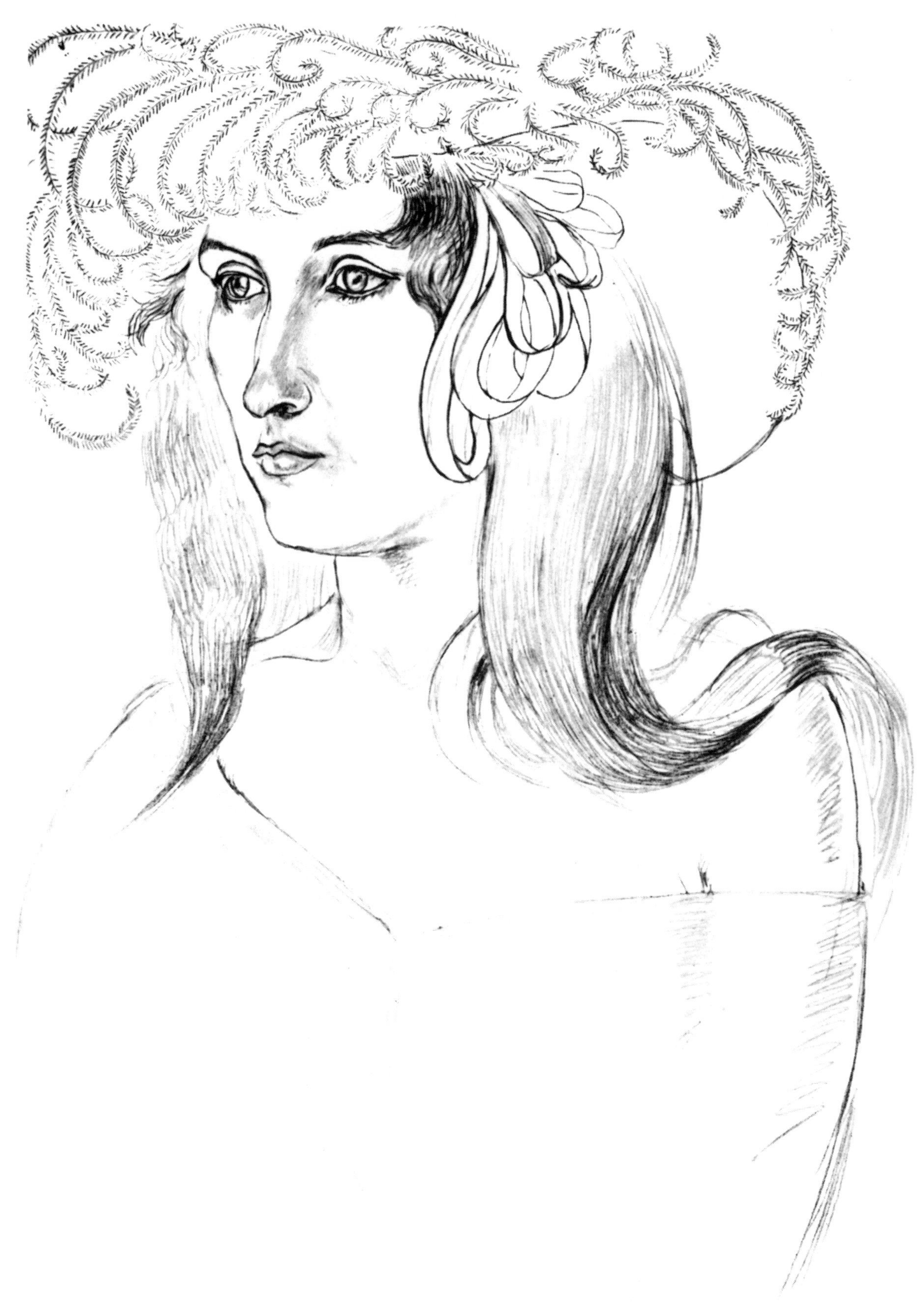

Study for *Les Plumes Blanches.* Pencil.

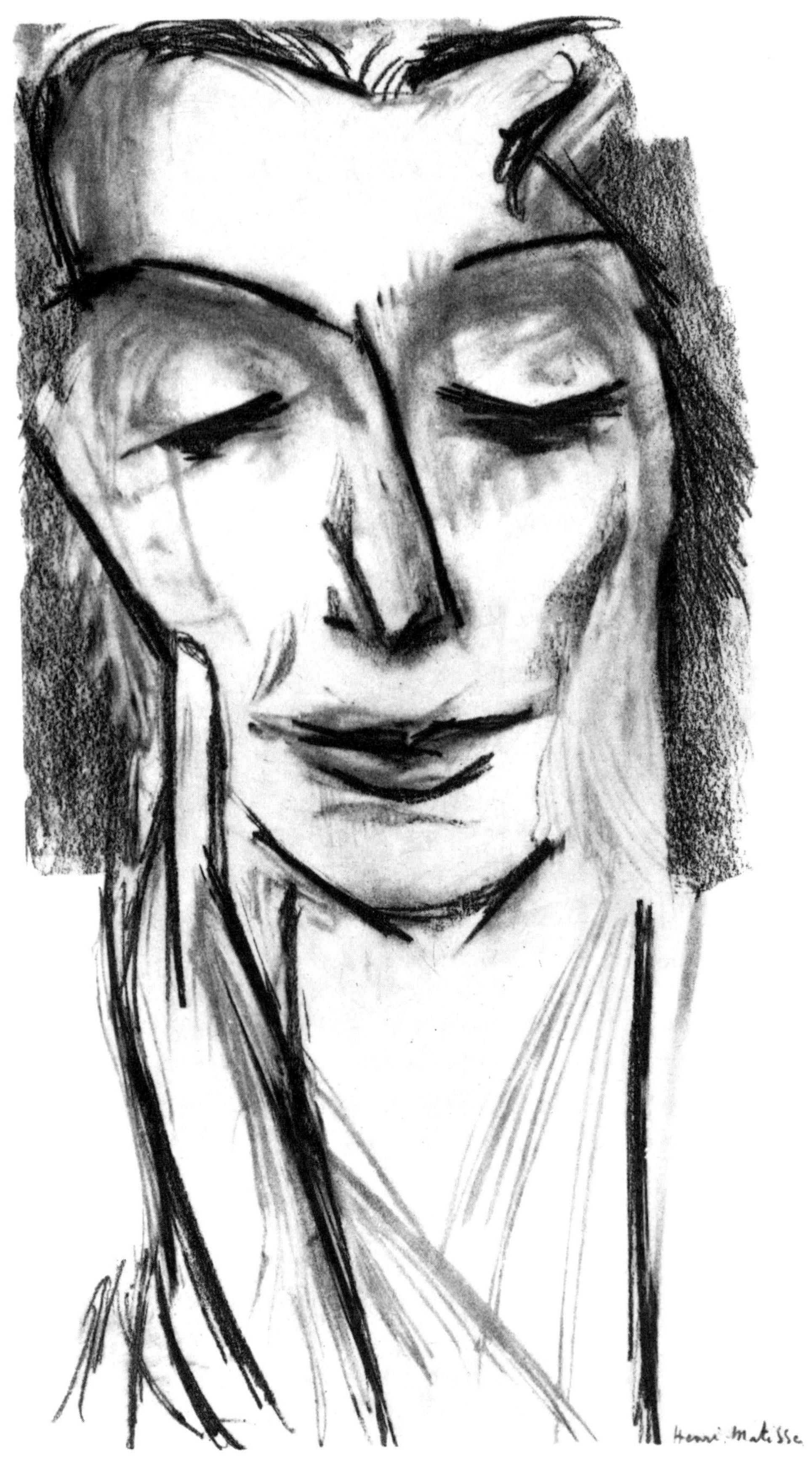

Josette Gris, 1915. Charcoal.

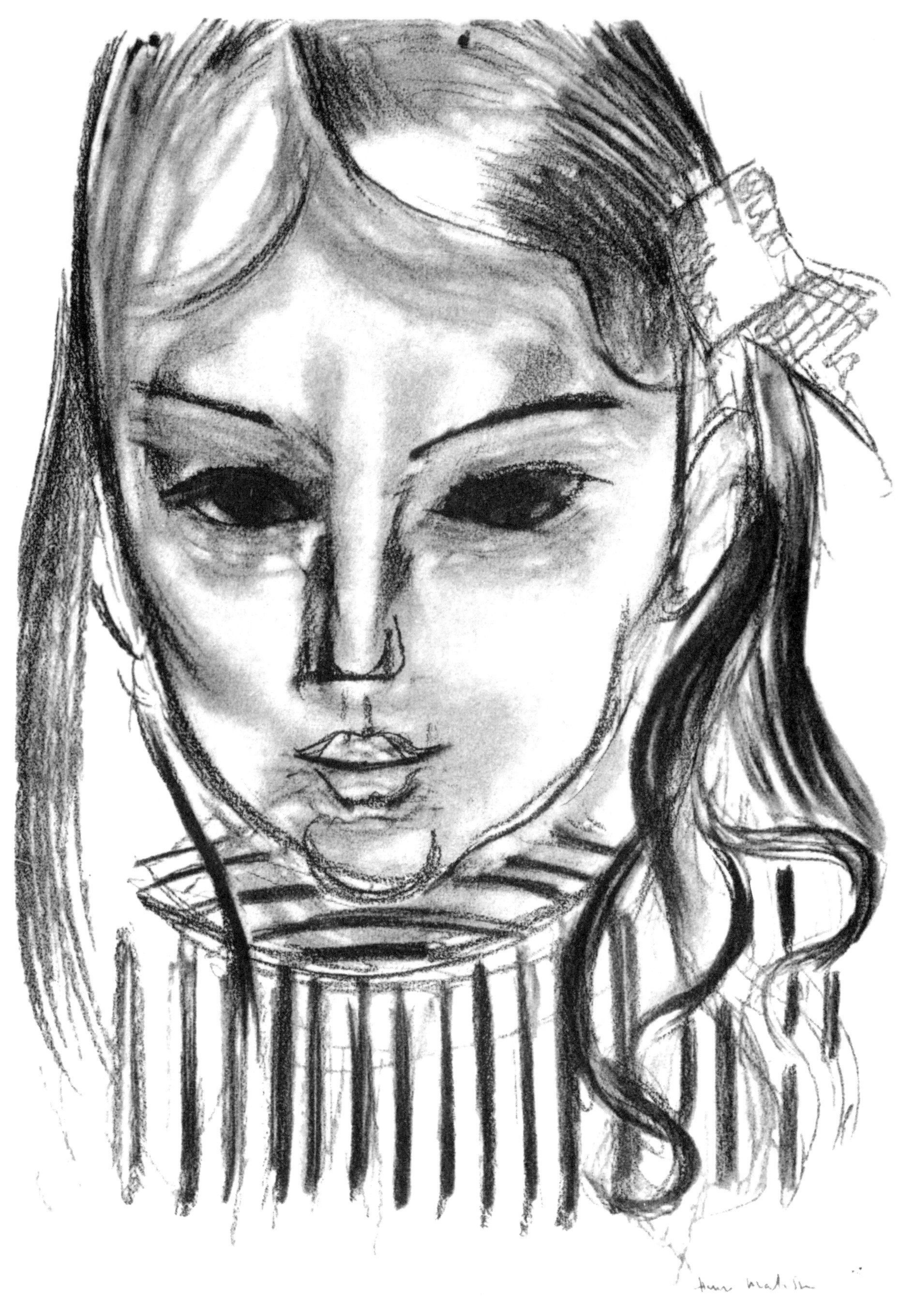

Cocoly Agelasto, 1915. Charcoal.

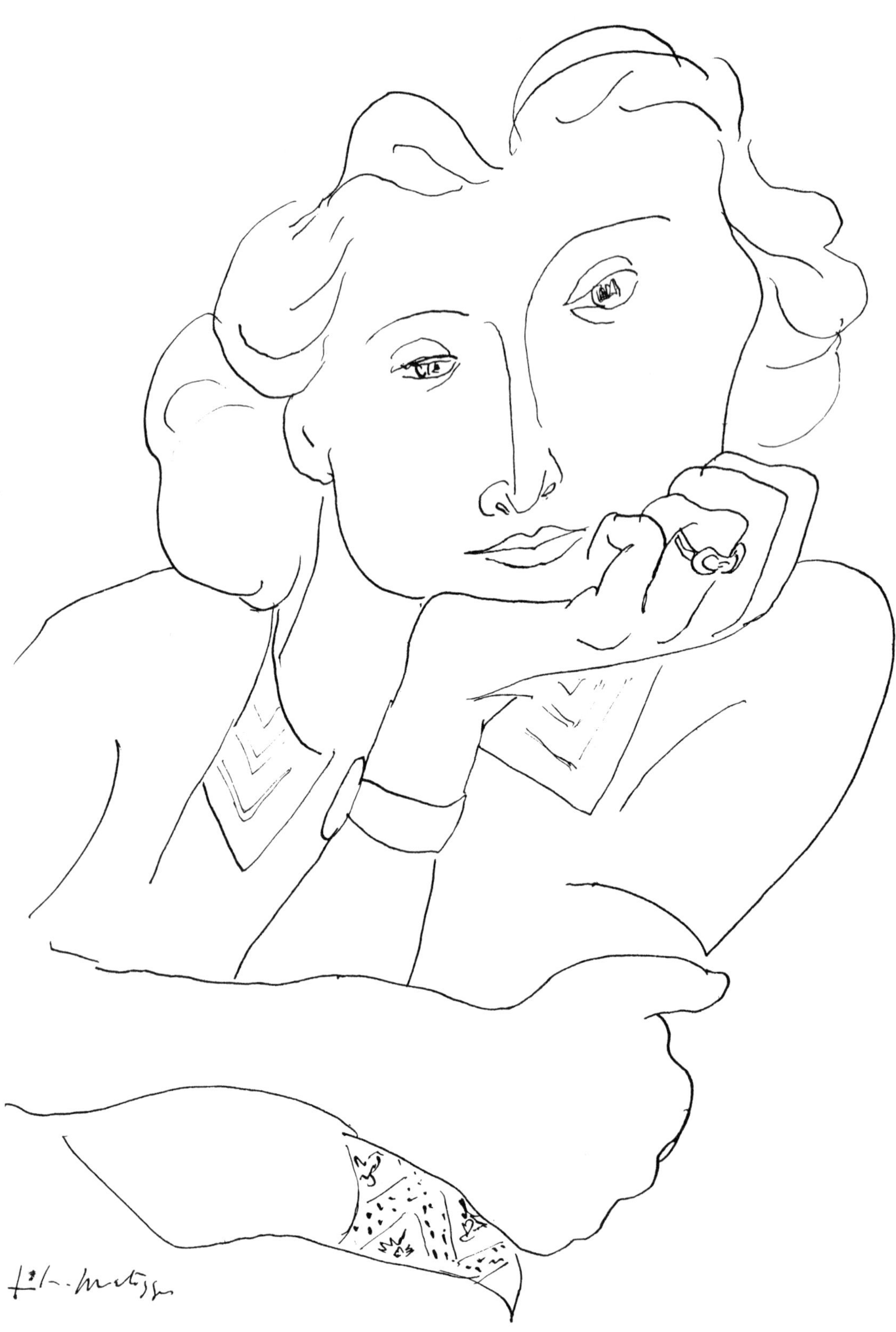

L. D., 1937. Pen and india ink, 38 × 28 cm.

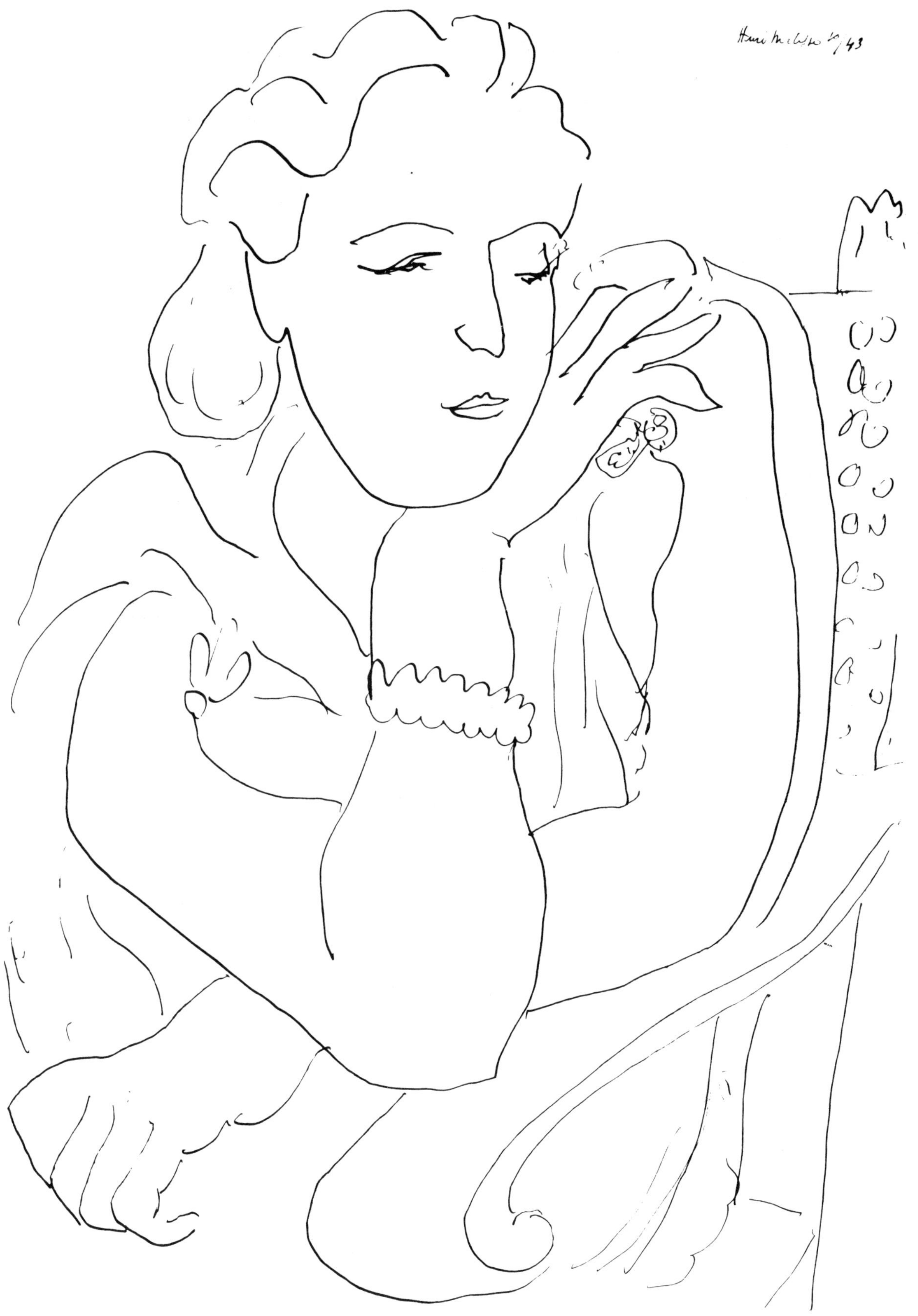

M. B., 1943. Pen and india ink, 49 × 37 cm.

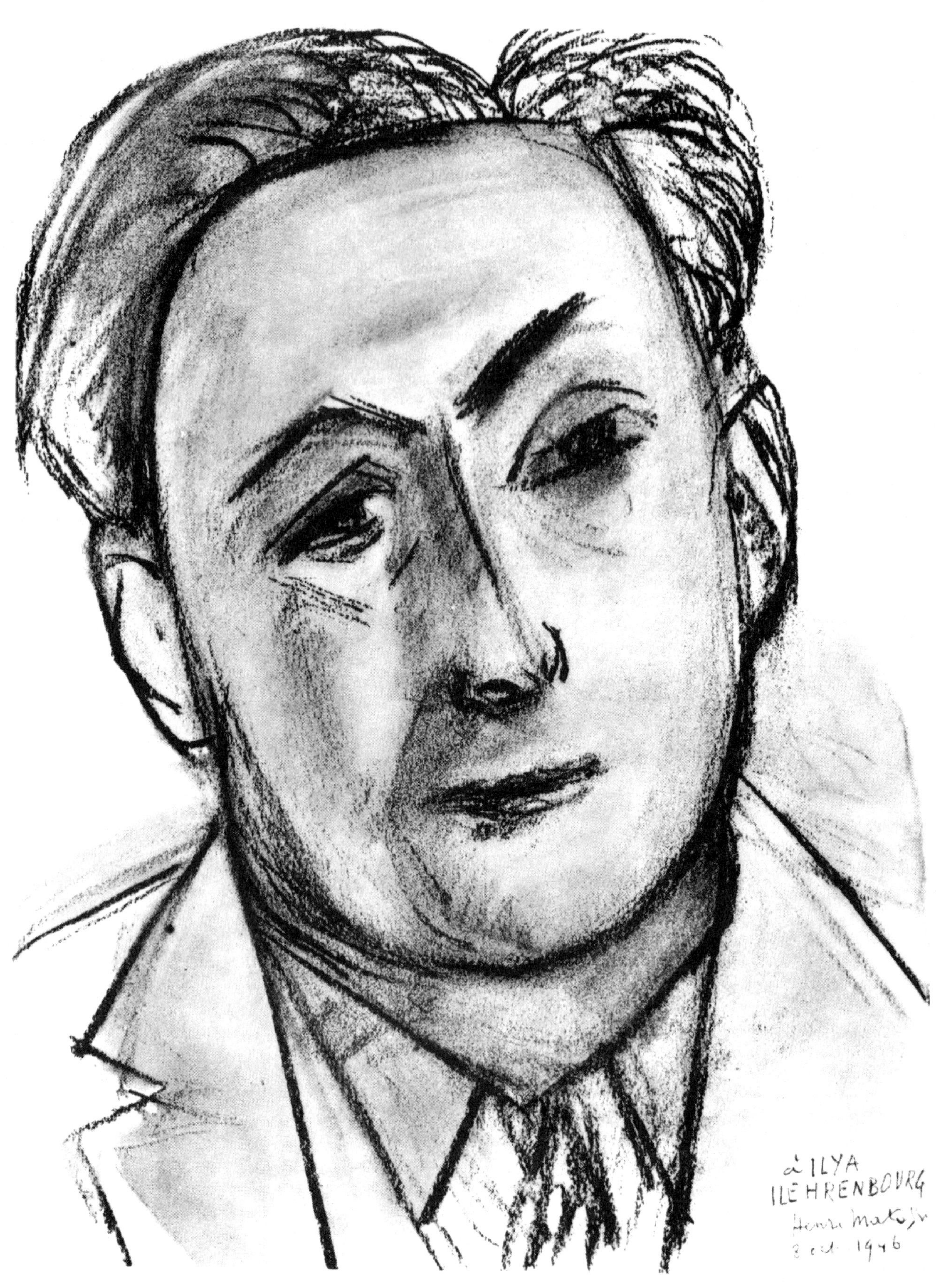

Ilya Ehrenburg (1891–1967), 1946. Charcoal, 42 × 32 cm.

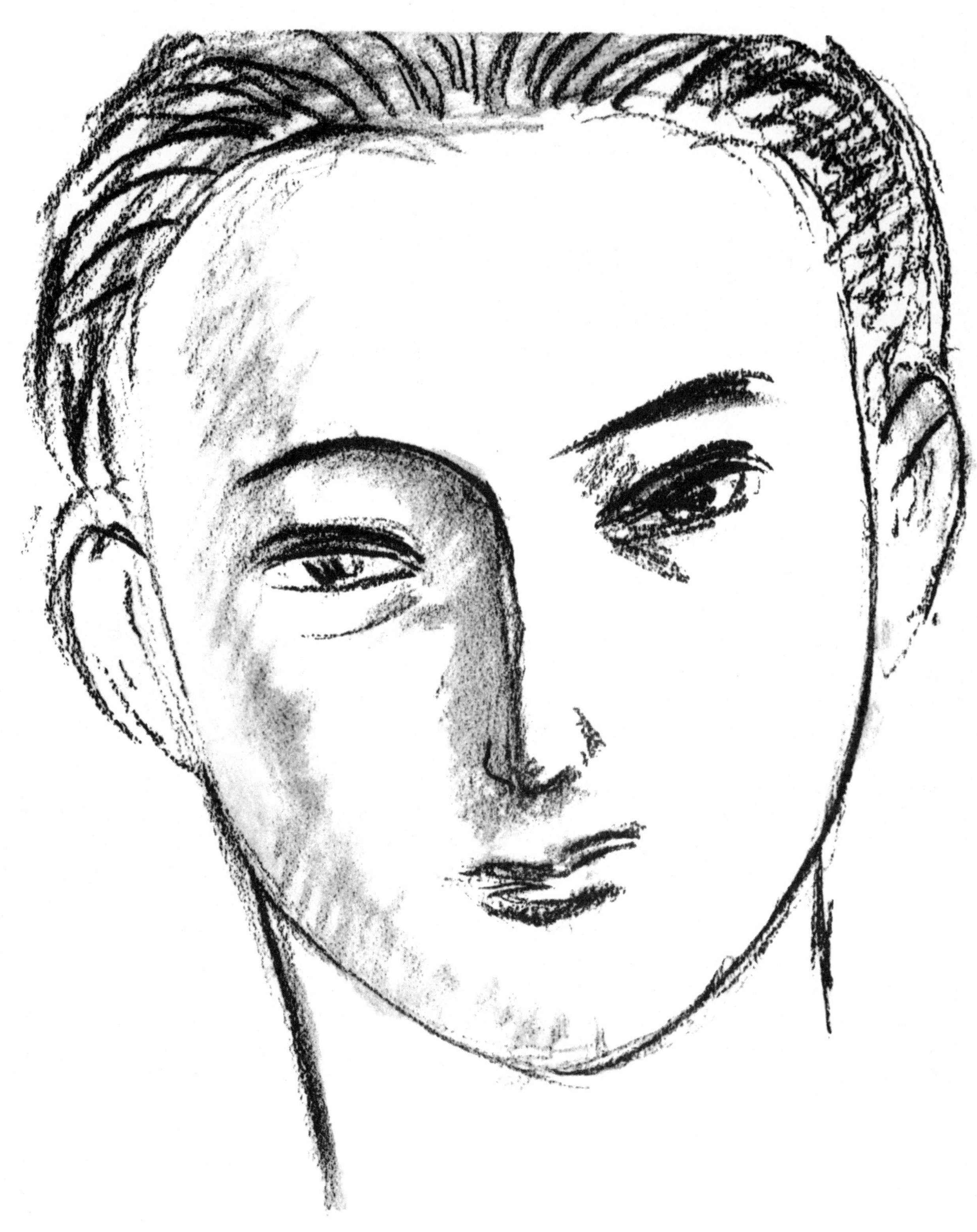

Ilya Ehrenburg (1891–1967), "after having seen the film *Notre Jeunesse*," 1946. Charcoal, 42 × 32 cm.

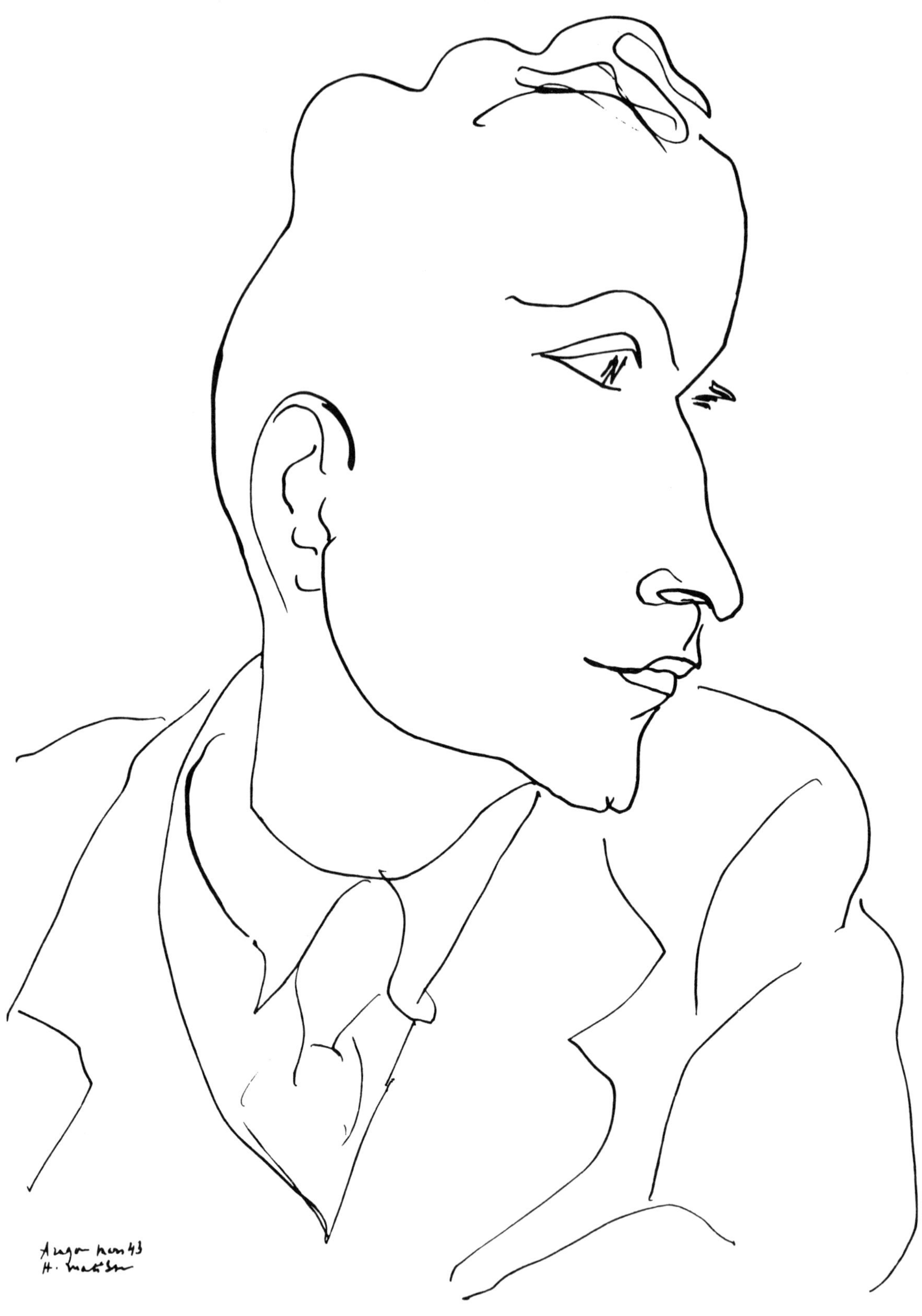

Louis Aragon (1897–1982), 1943. Pen and india ink, 52 × 40 cm.

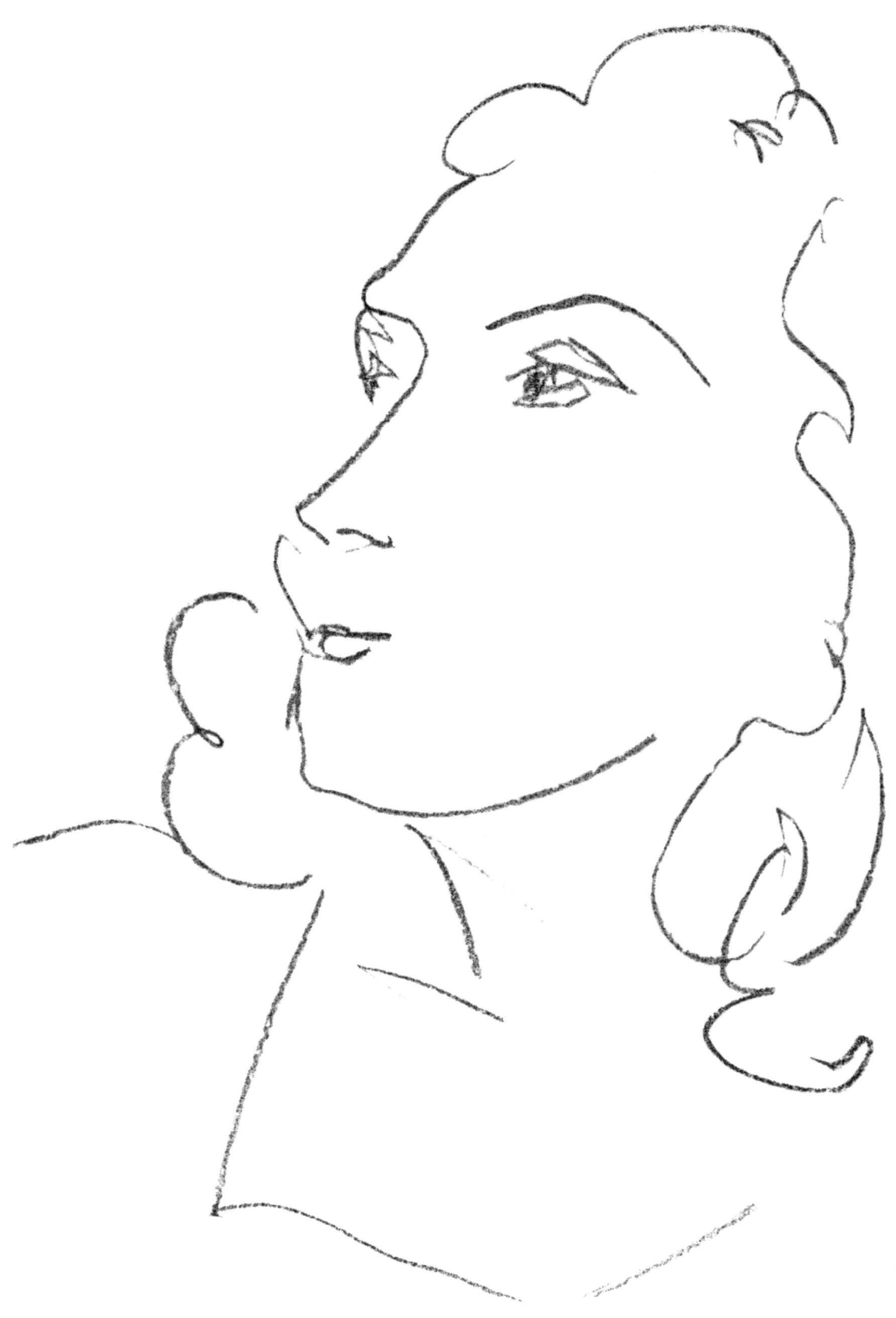

Elsa Triolet, 1946. Lithographic crayon, 36 × 26 cm.

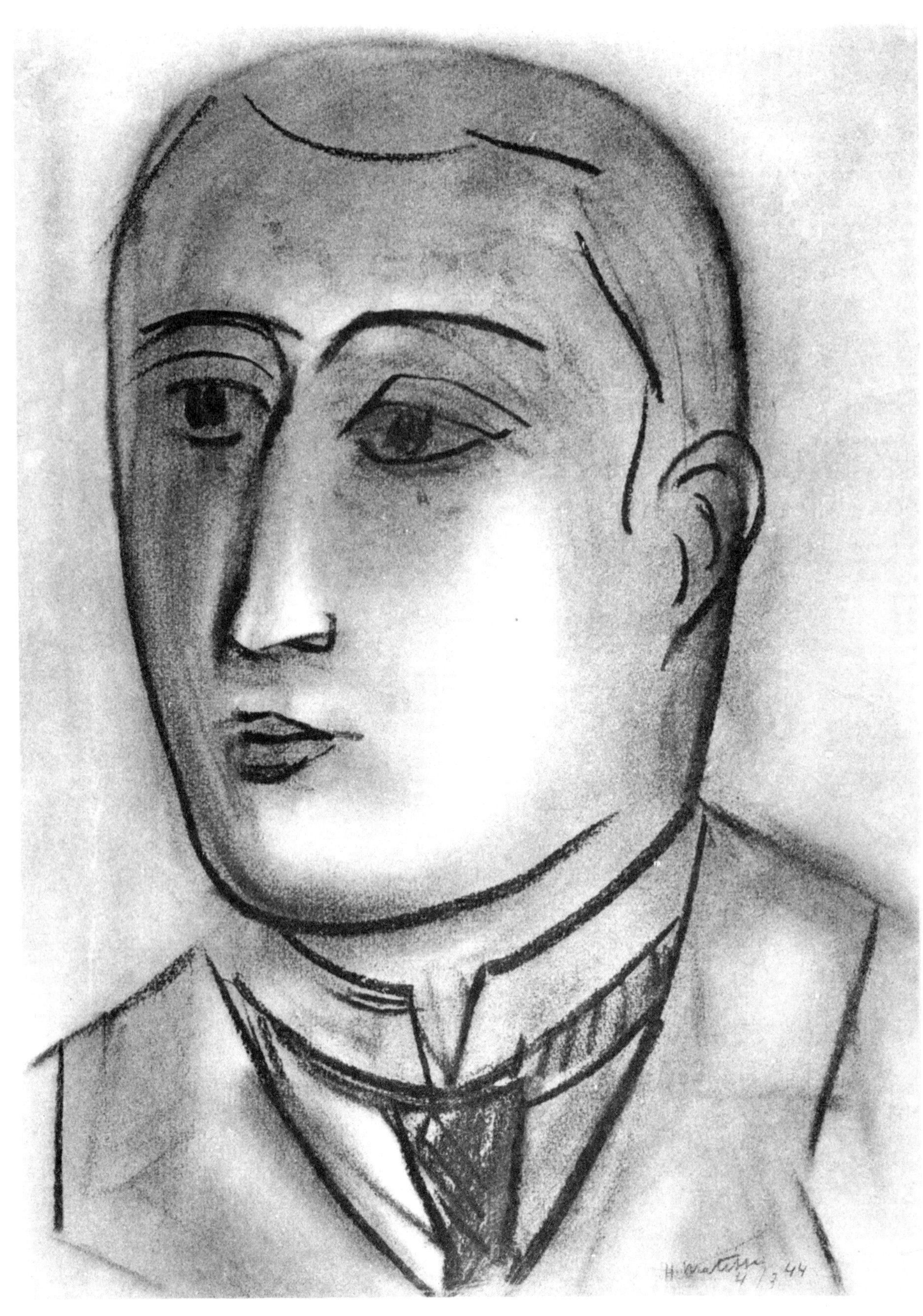

Guillaume Apollinaire (1880–1918), 1944. Charcoal.

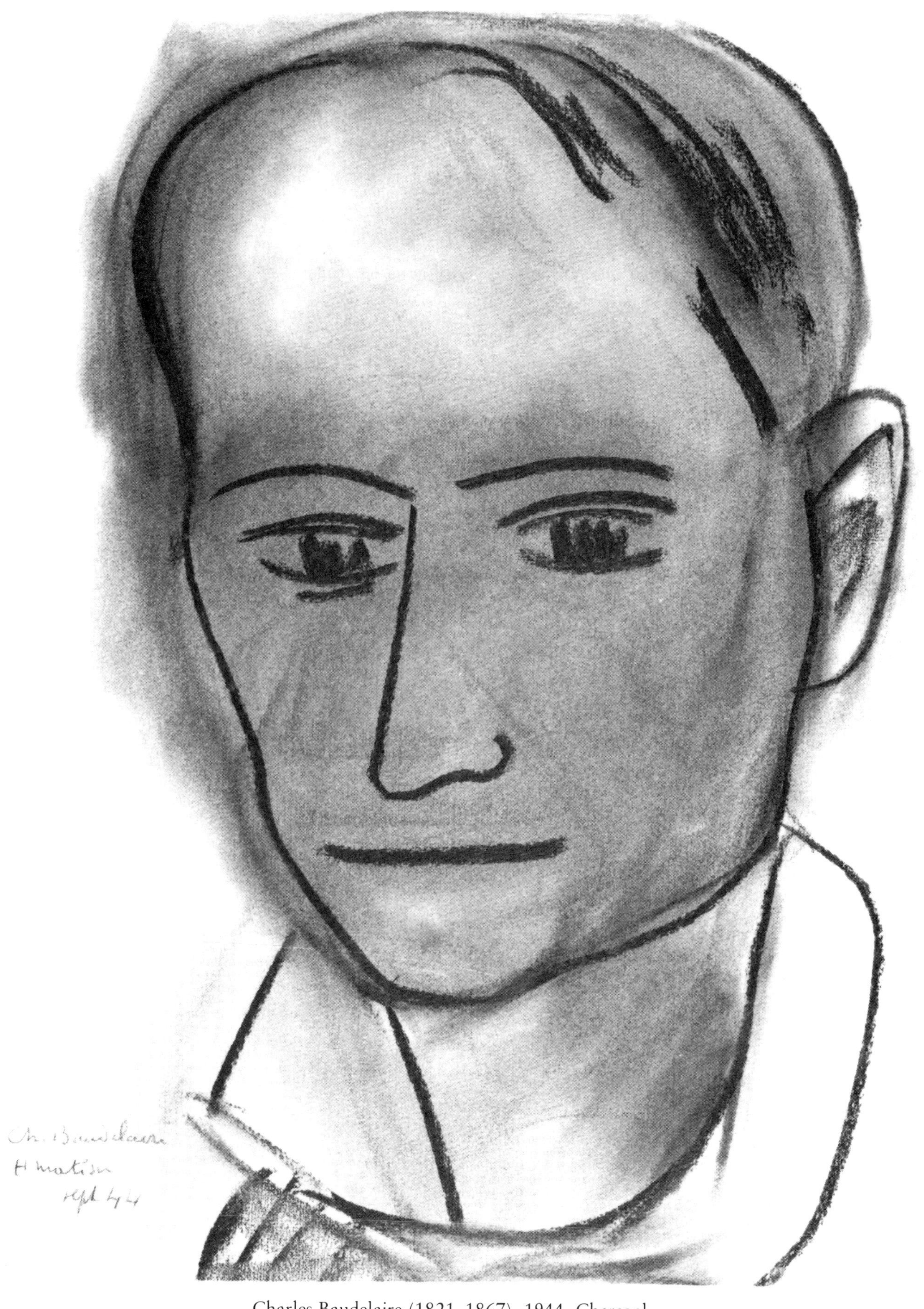

Charles Baudelaire (1821–1867), 1944. Charcoal.

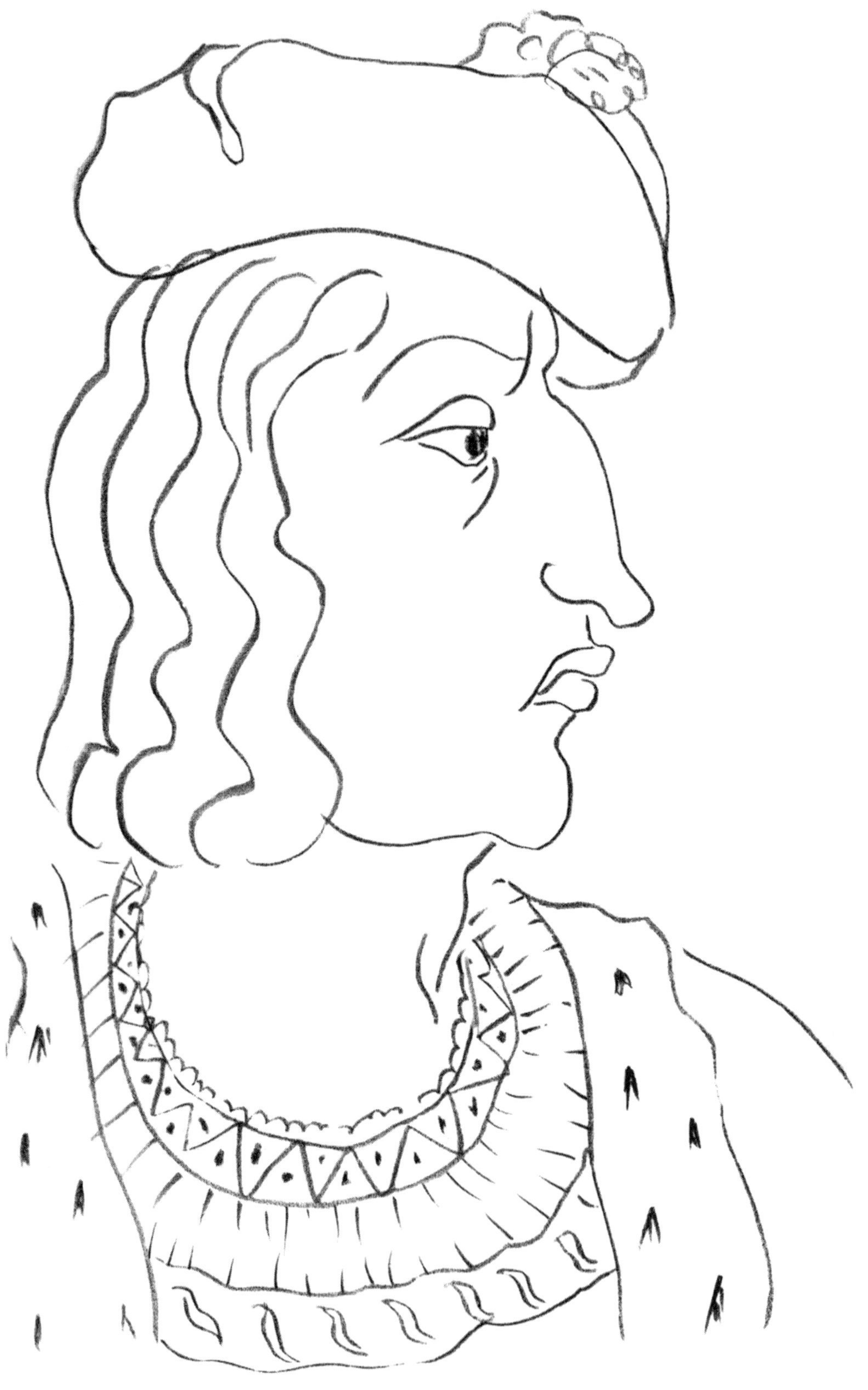

Charles d'Orléans (1394–1465), 1943. Conté crayon, 40 × 26 cm.

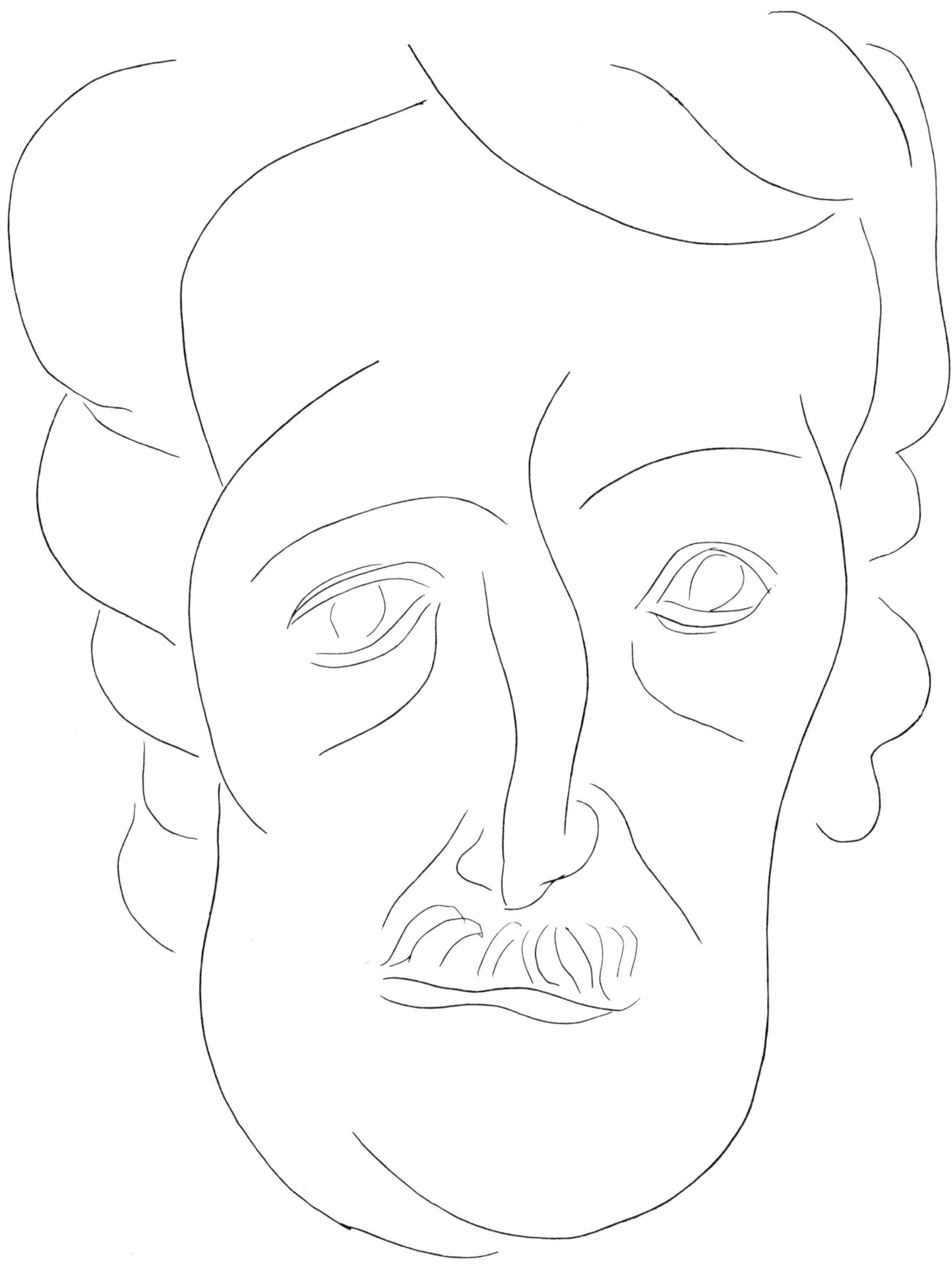

Edgar Allan Poe (1809–1849), 1931. Etching, 33 × 25 cm.

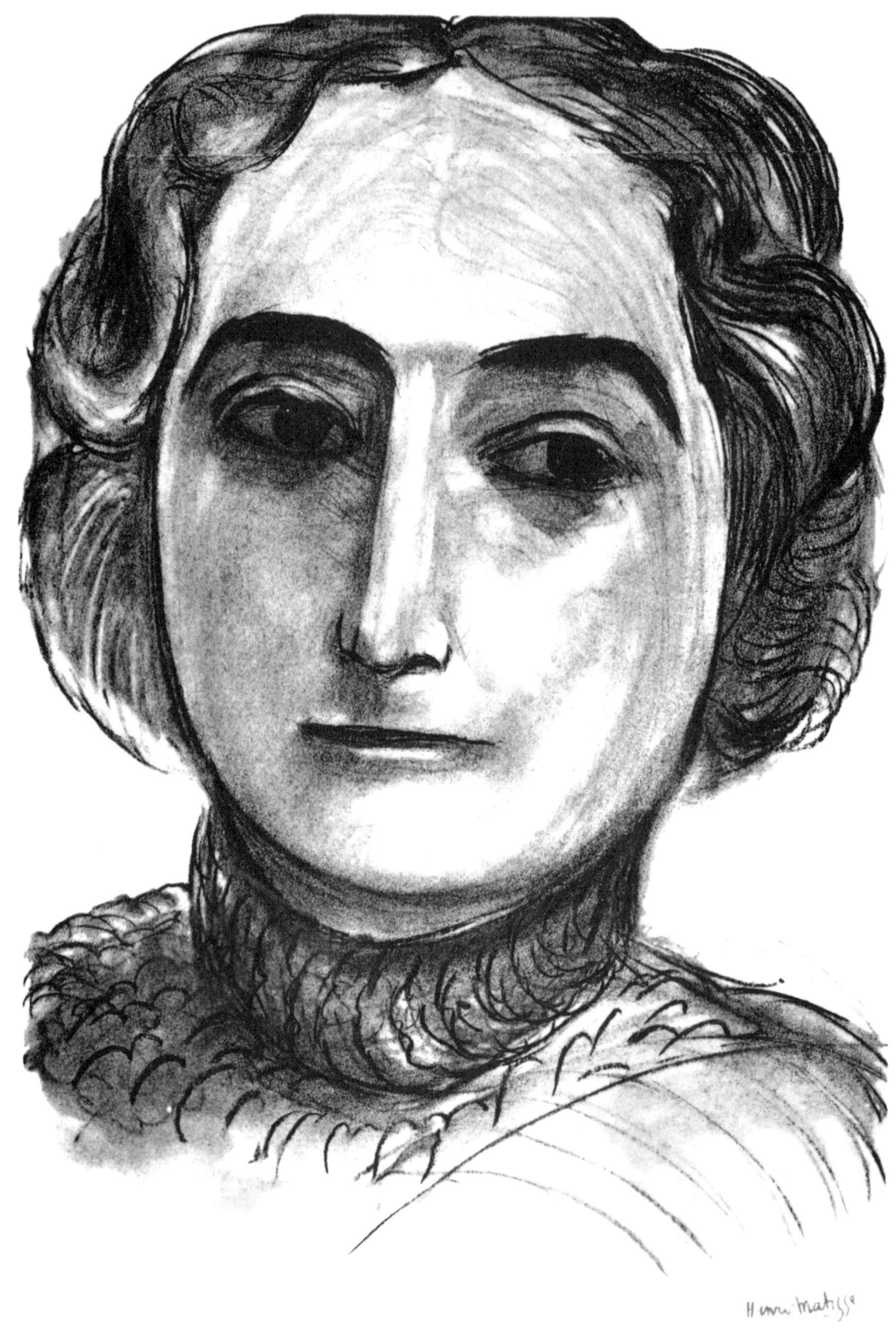

Claribel Cone, 1933. Charcoal, 59 × 41 cm.

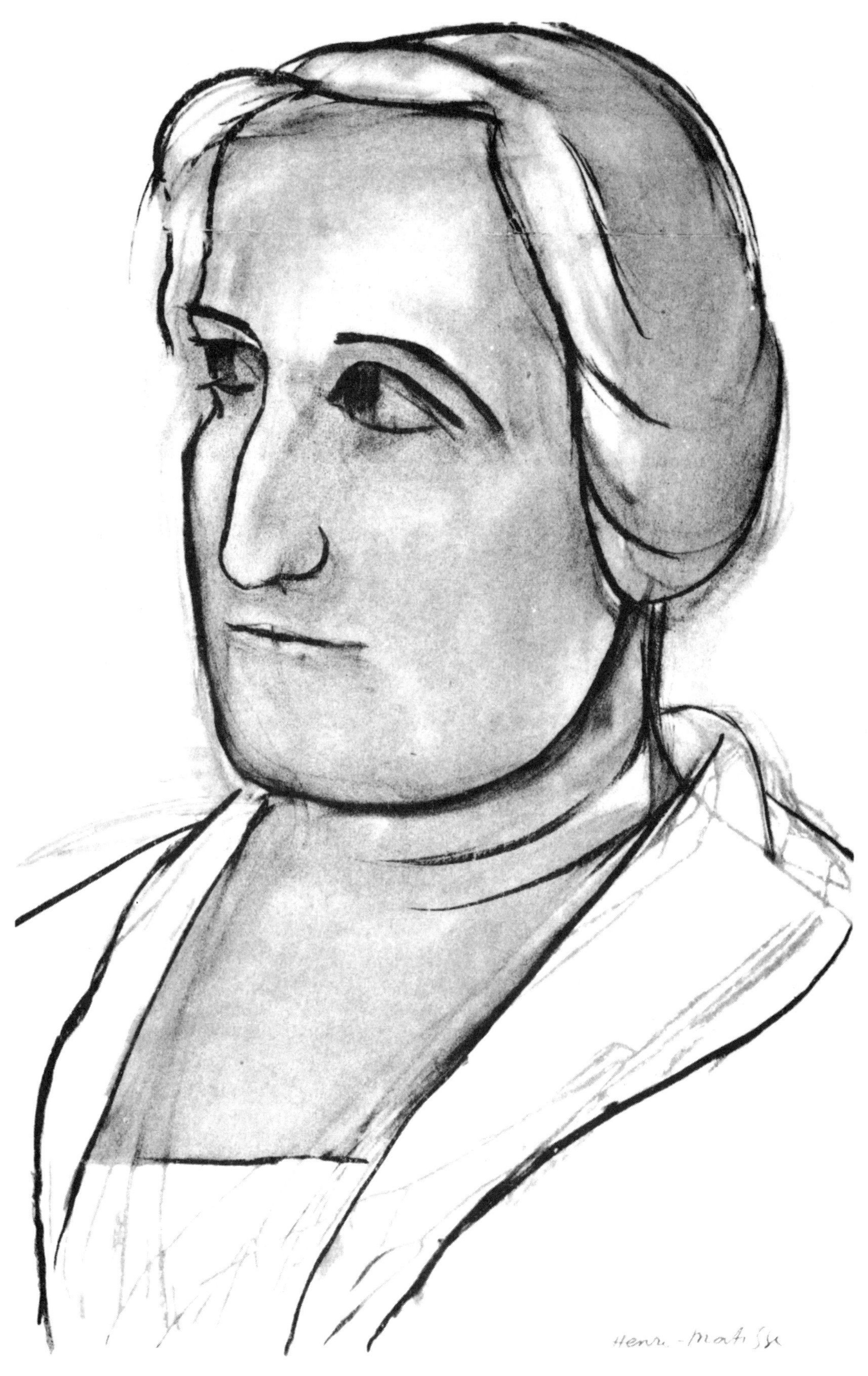

Etta Cone, 1934. Charcoal, 62 × 40 cm.

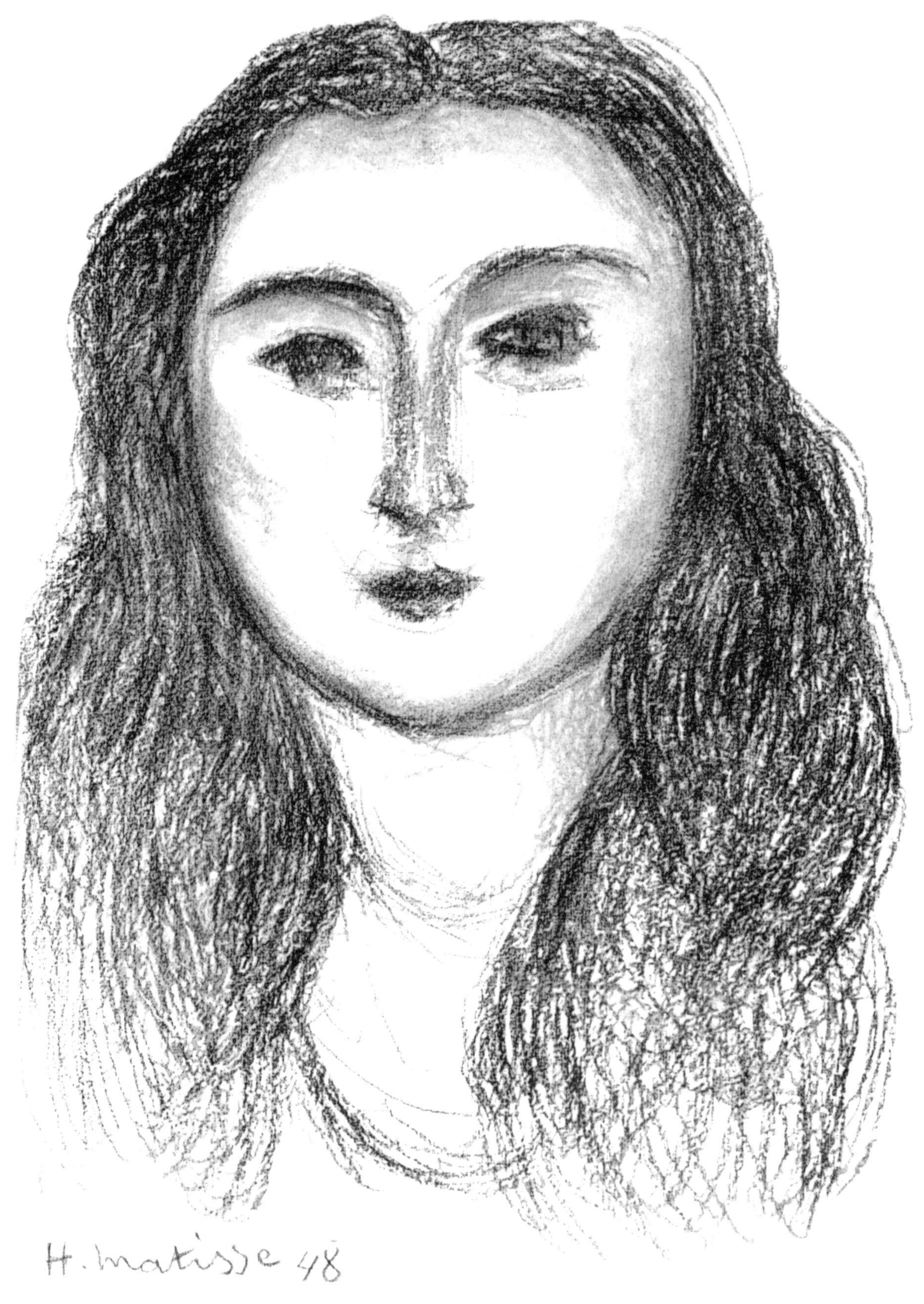

Nadia Sednaoui, 1948. Charcoal, 40.5 × 30 cm.

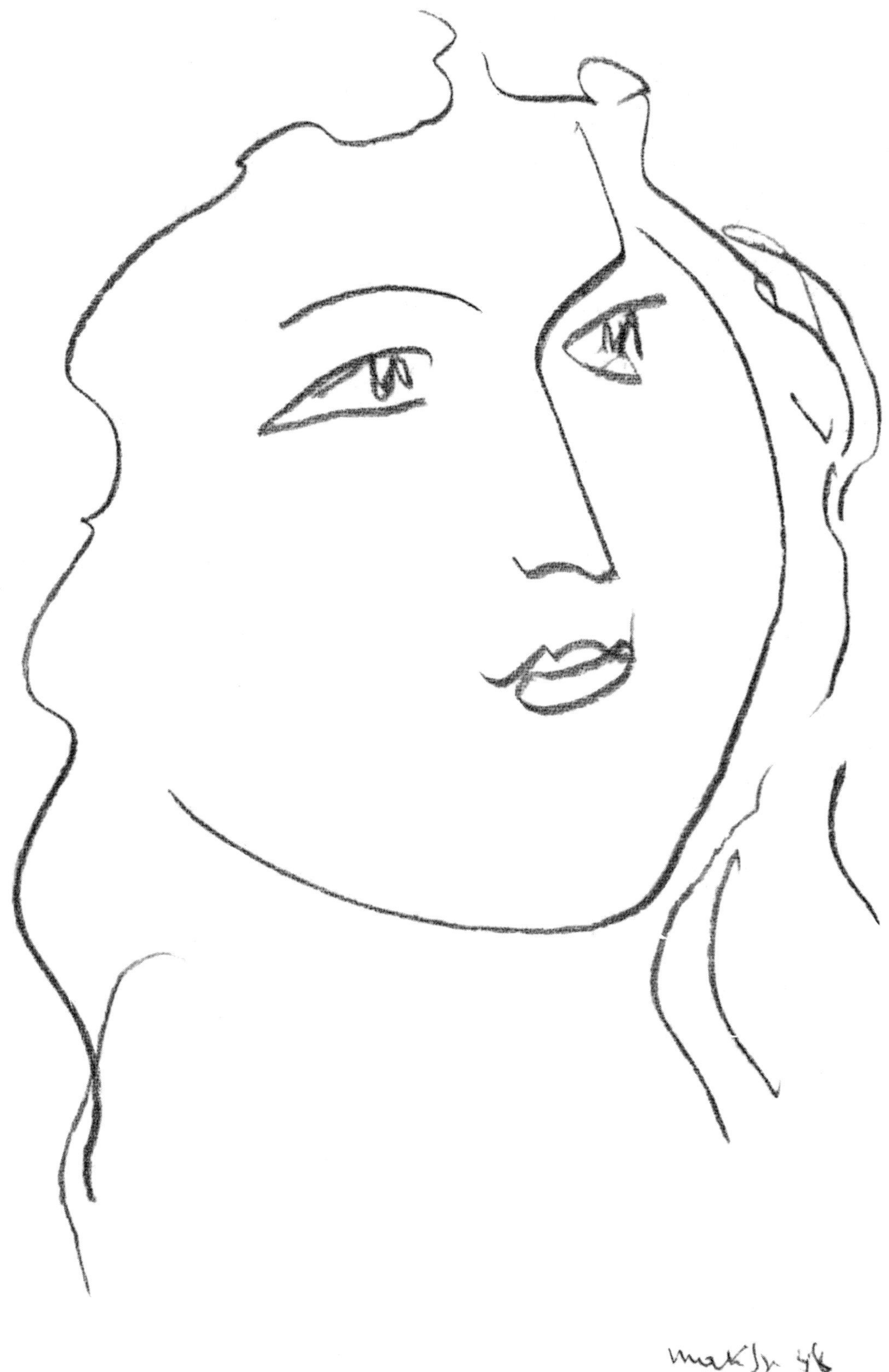

Nadia Sednaoui, 1948. Conté crayon.

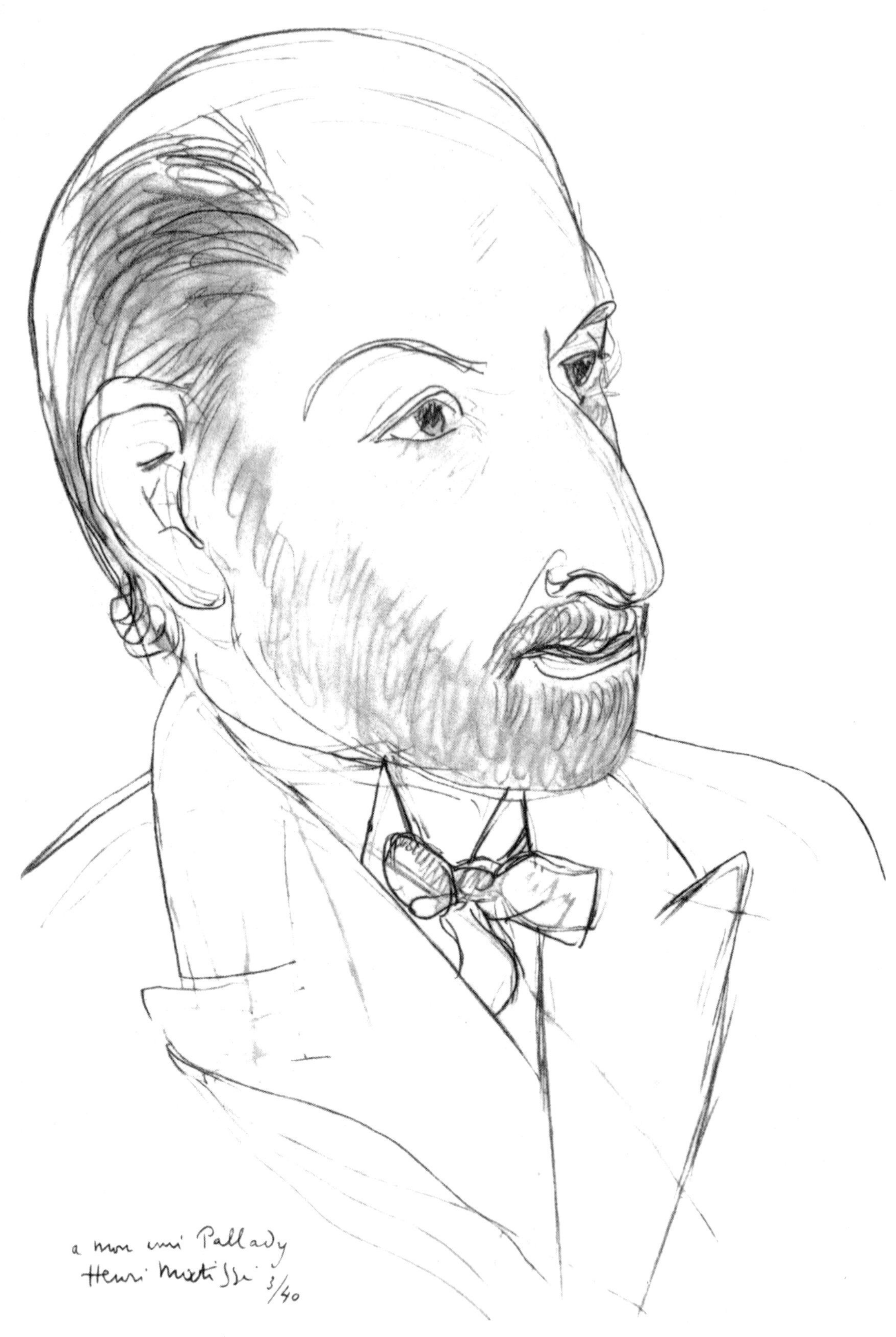

Theodore Pallady (1871–1956), 1939. Pencil.

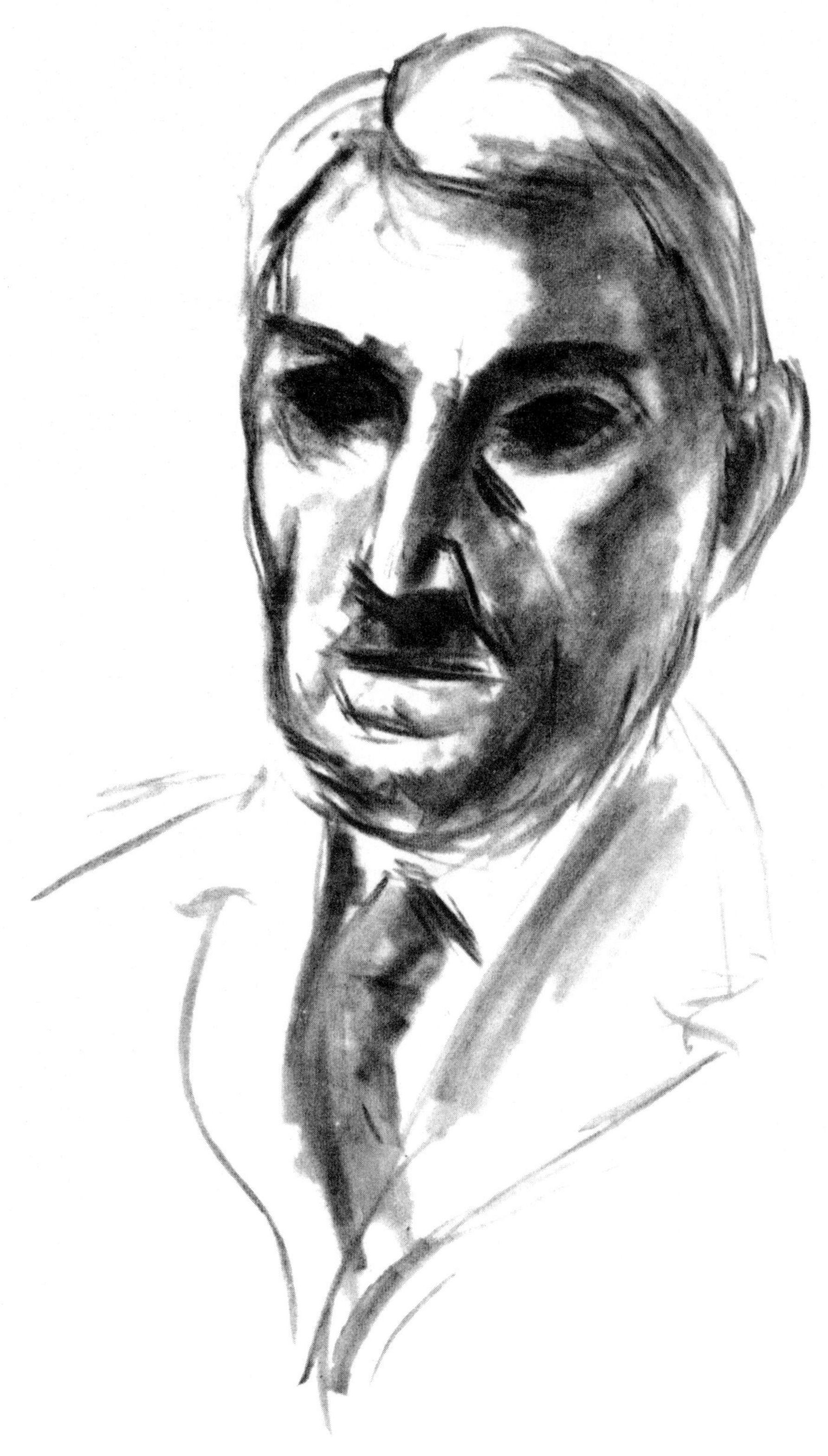

John Dewey (1859–1952), 1934. Stump drawing, 64 × 48 cm.

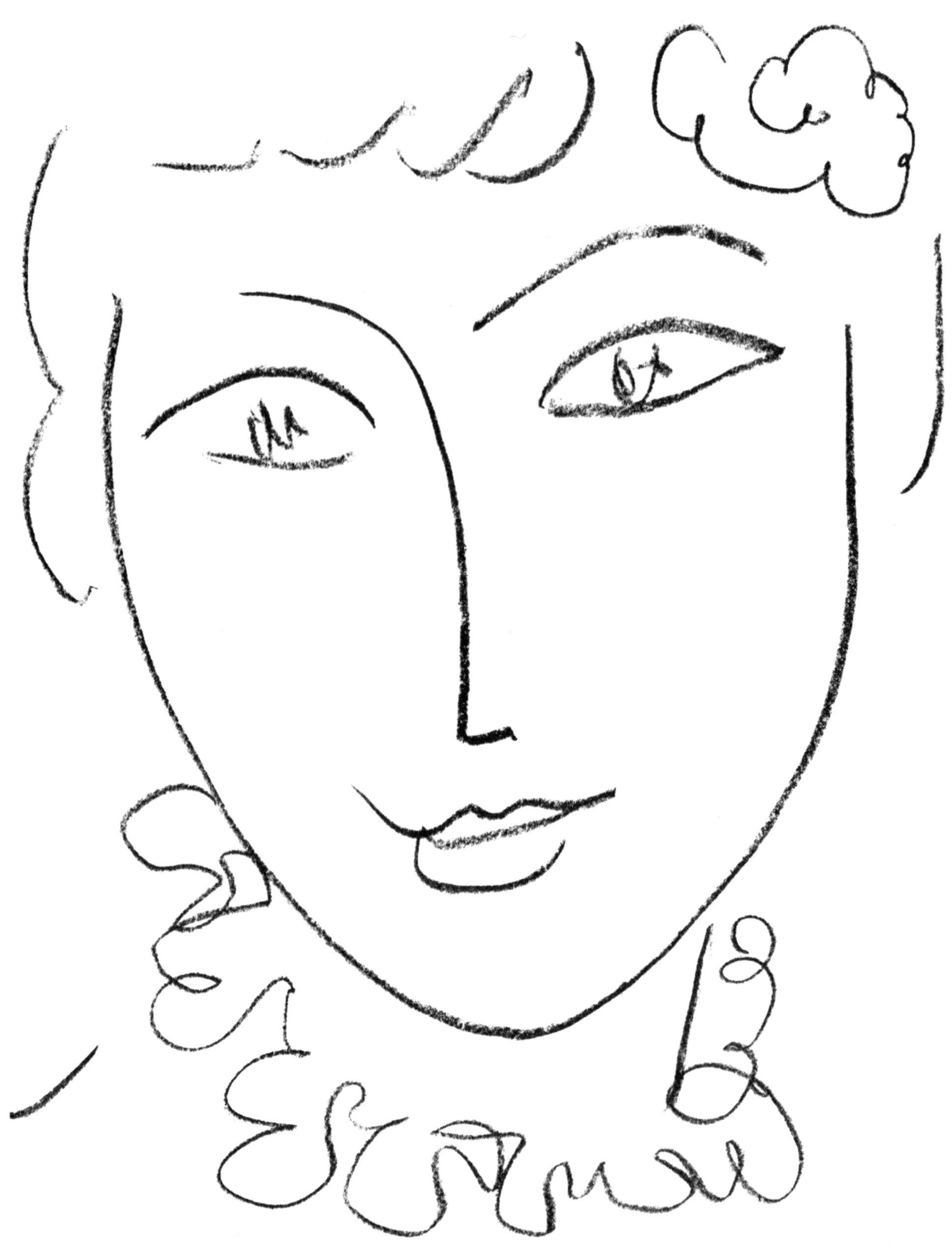

Lithograph, 31.3 × 24.5 cm.

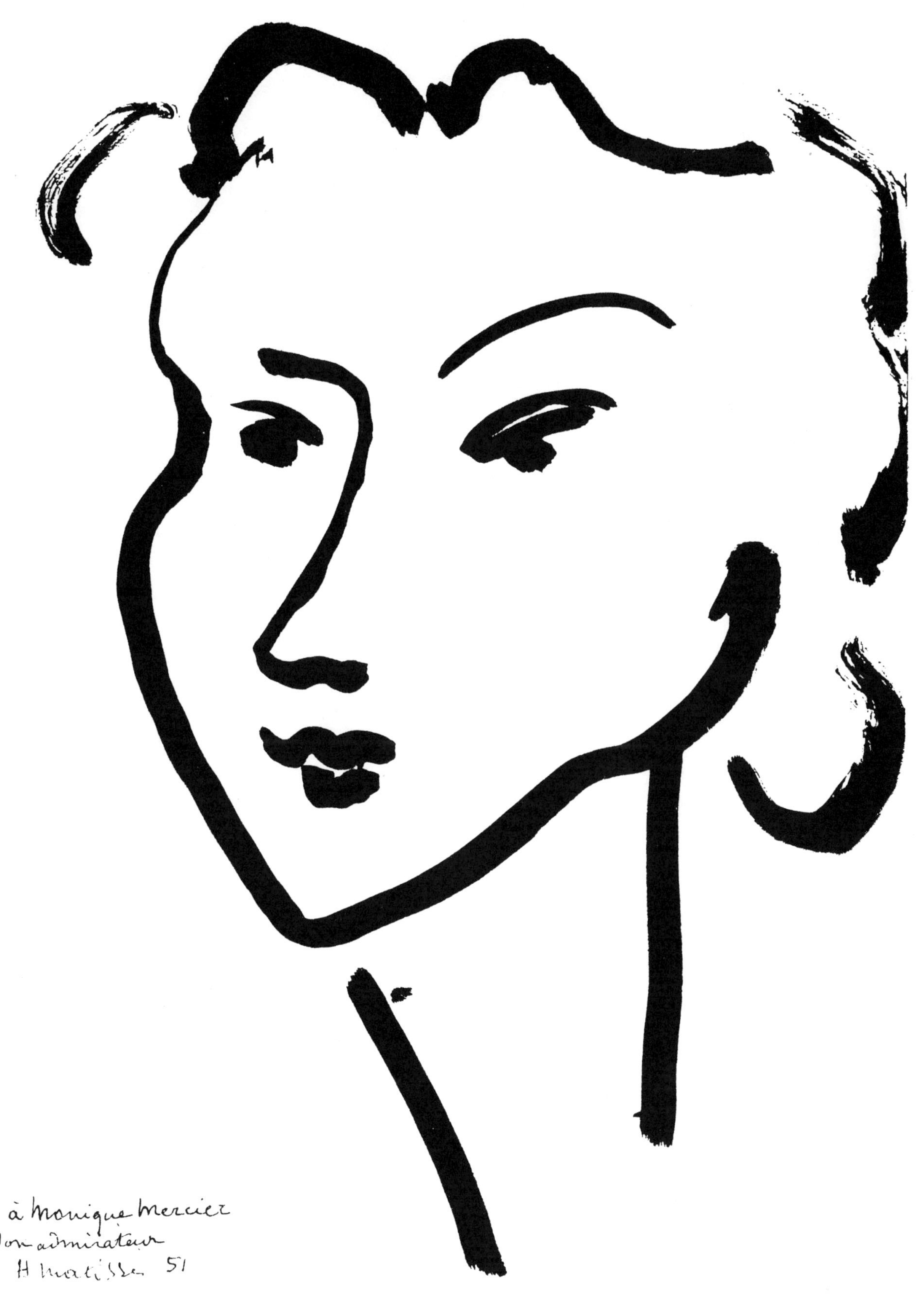

Monique Mercier, 1951. Brush and india ink.

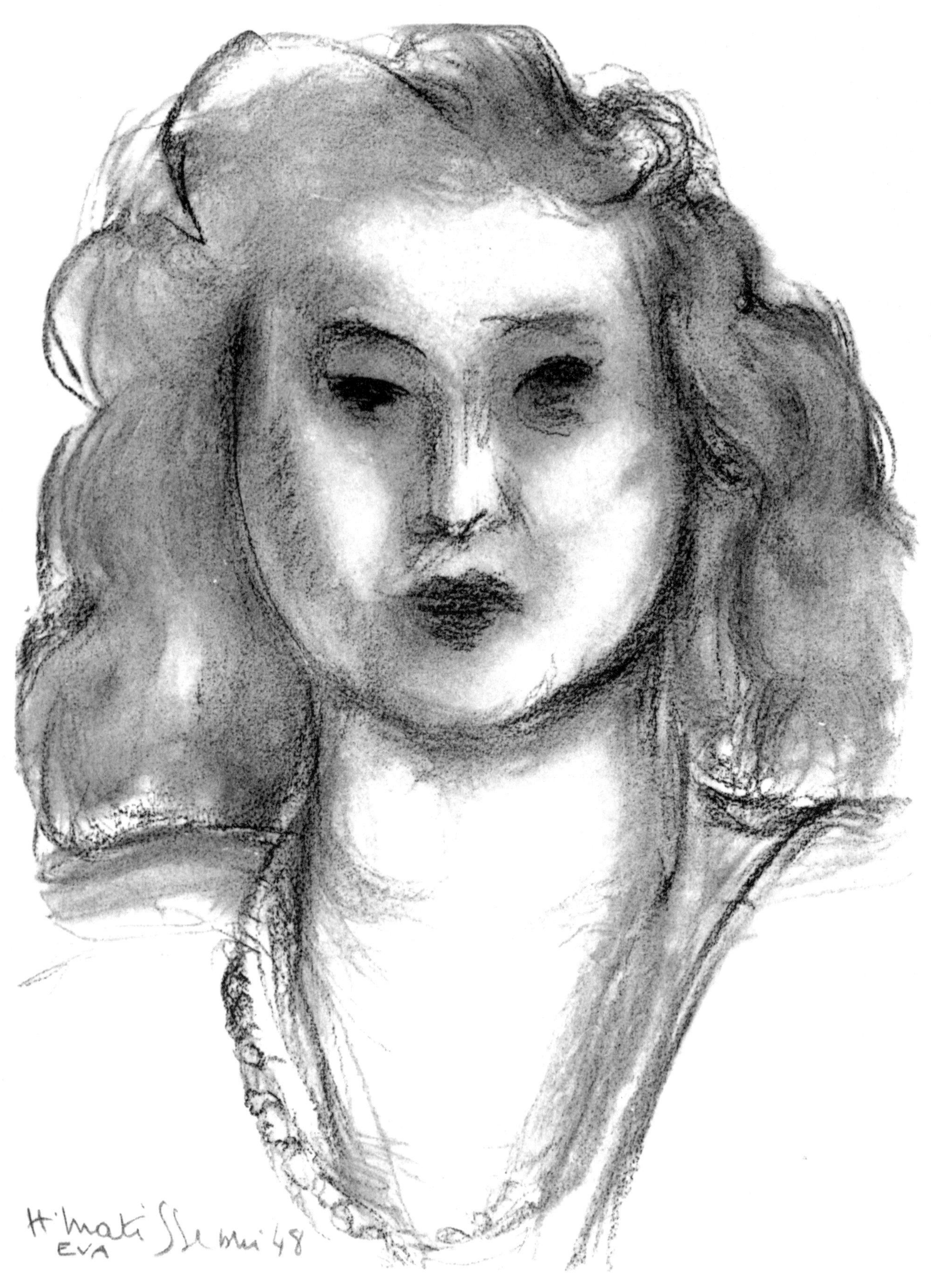

Vava Duclos, 1948. Charcoal.

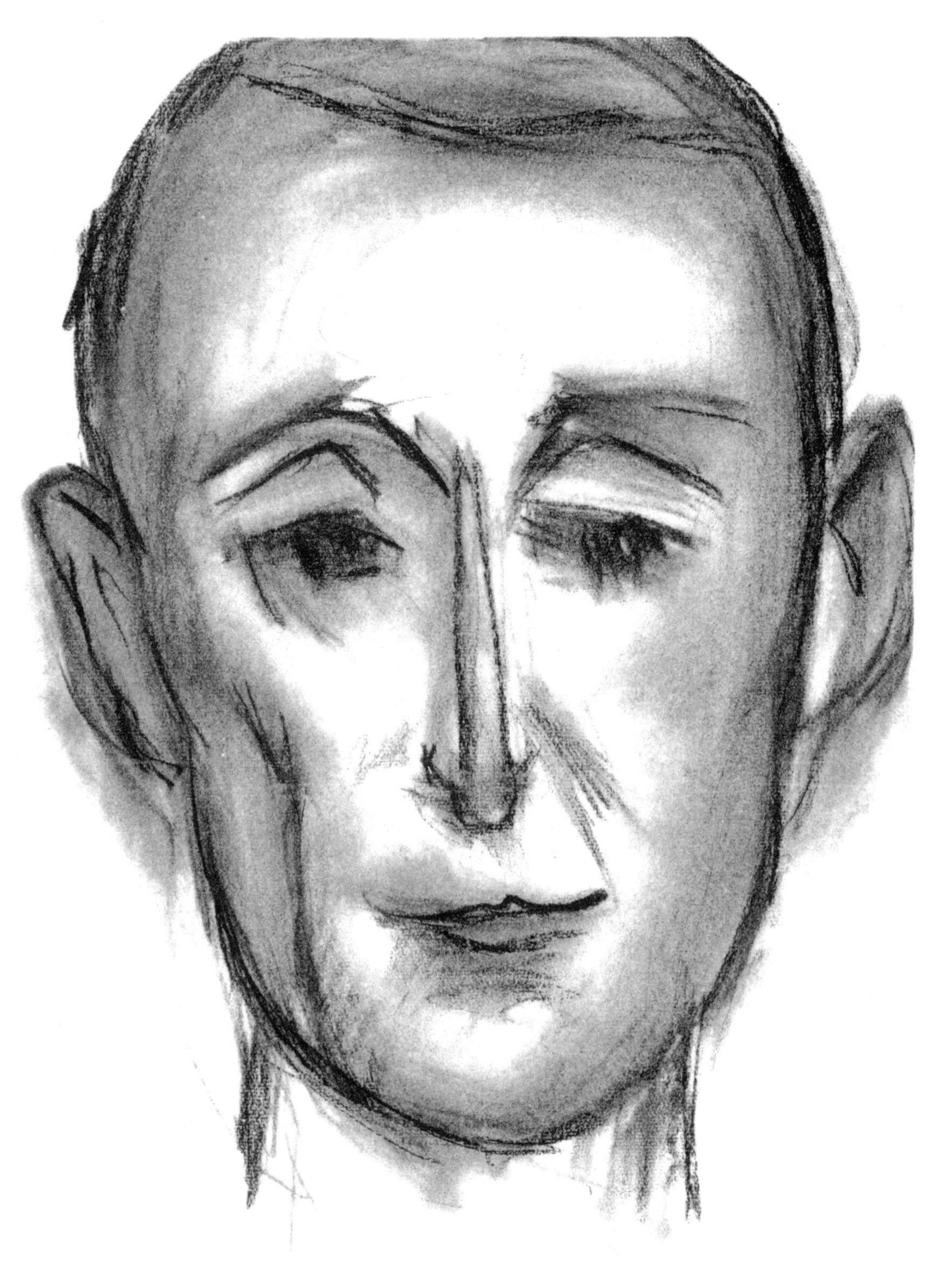

Albert Skira (1904–1973), 1948. Charcoal, 48 × 31.5 cm.

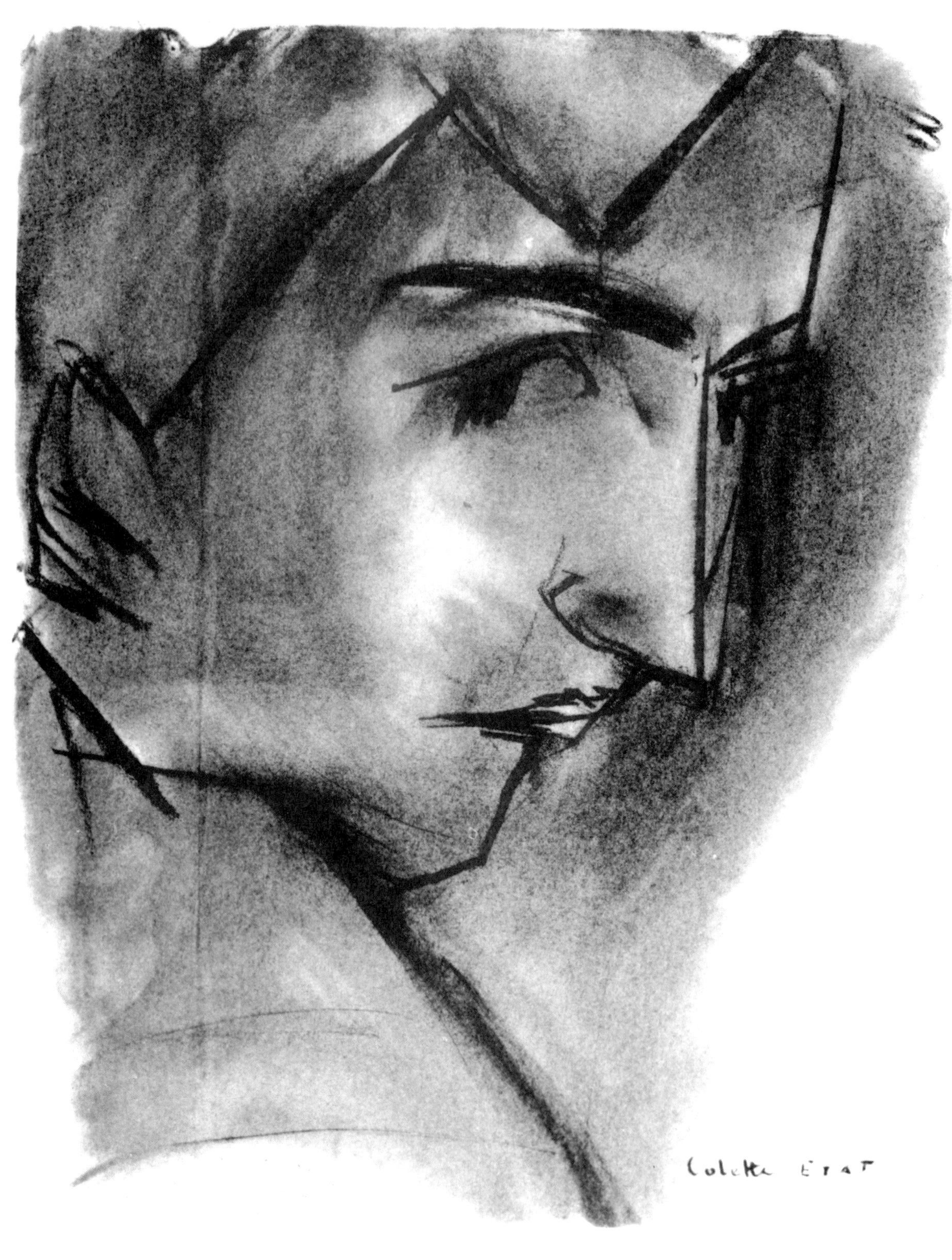

Colette (1873–1954), 1951. Charcoal, 52 × 40 cm.

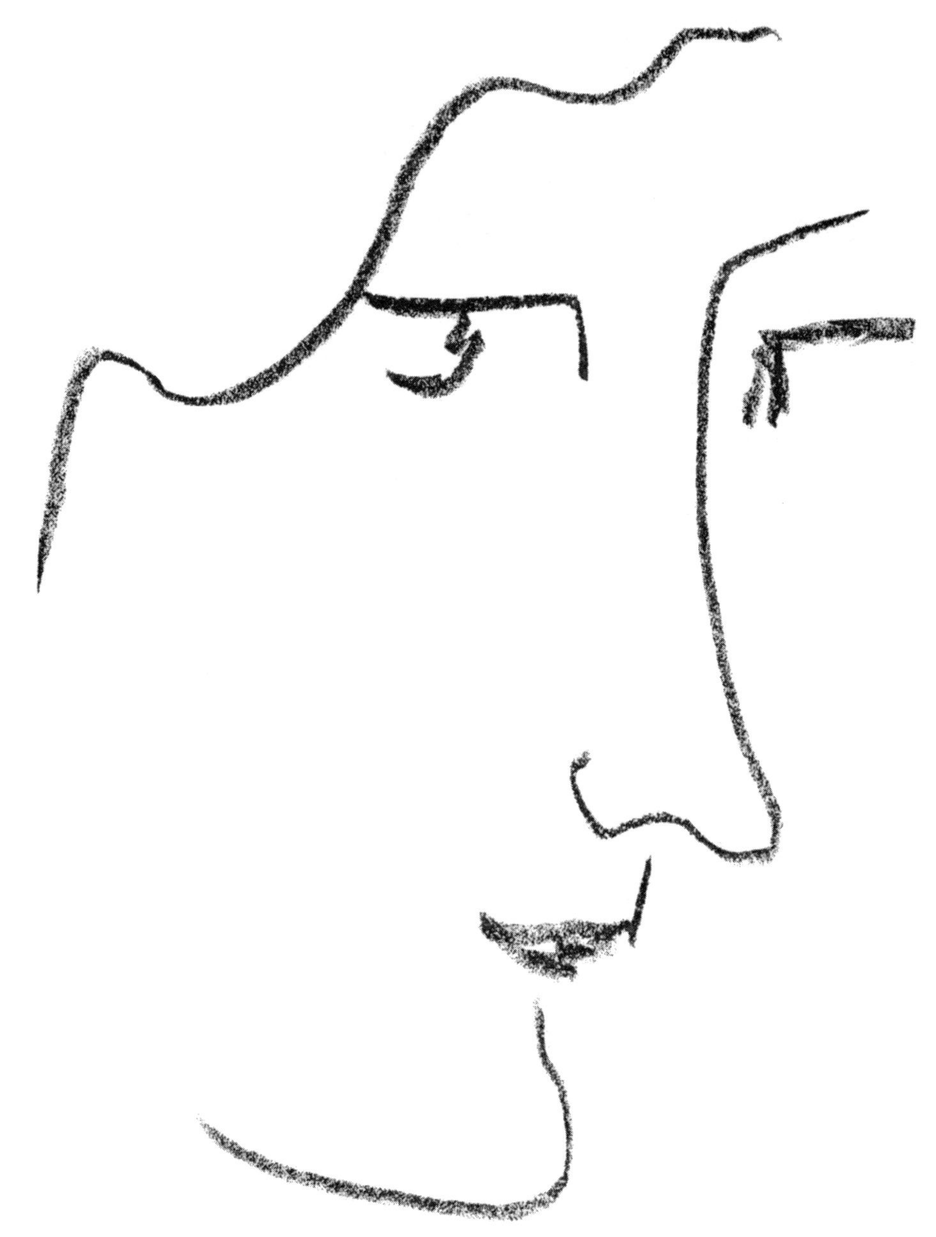

Colette (1873–1954), 1951. Lithograph, 22 × 16 cm.

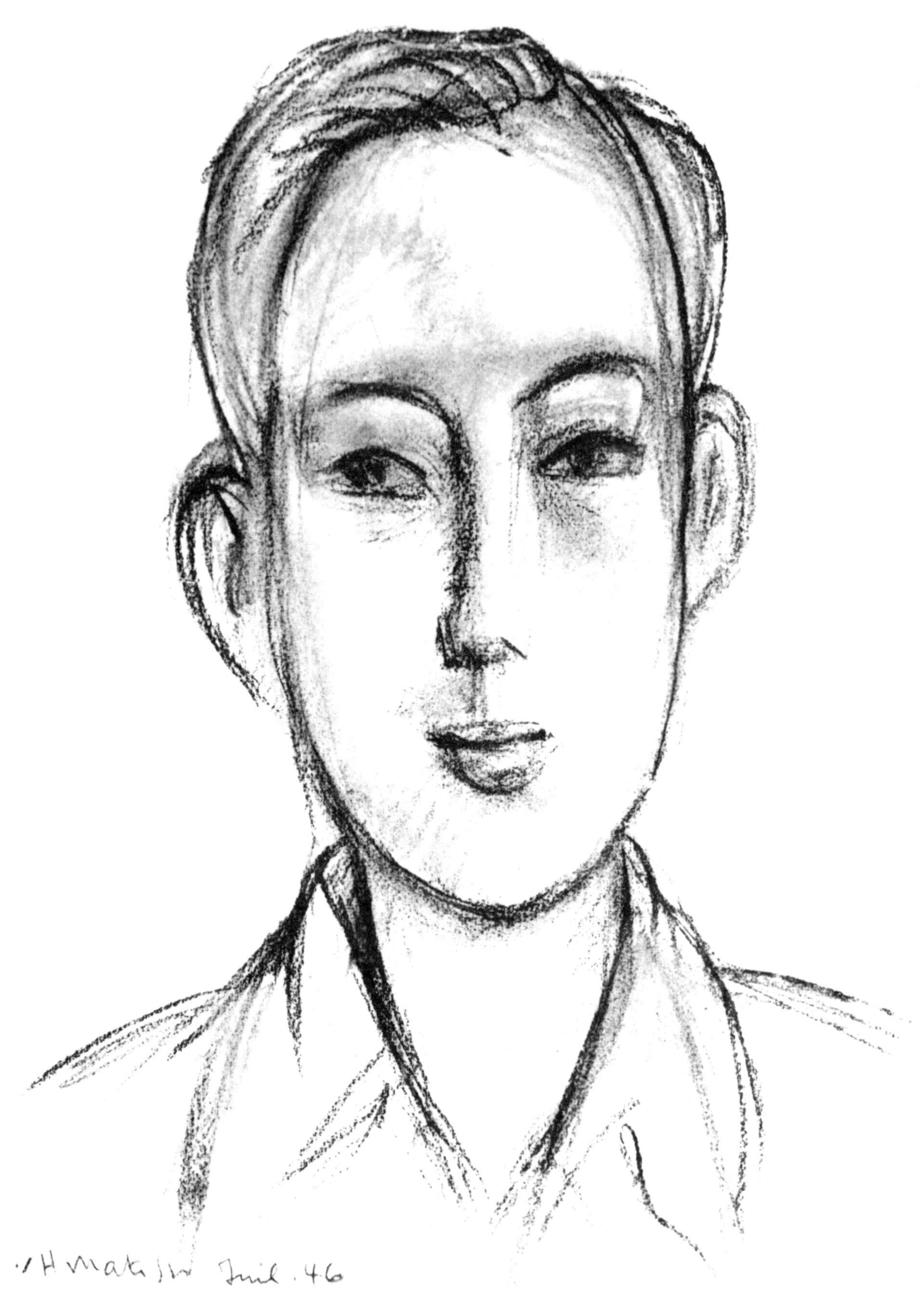

Paul Matisse, 1946. Charcoal.

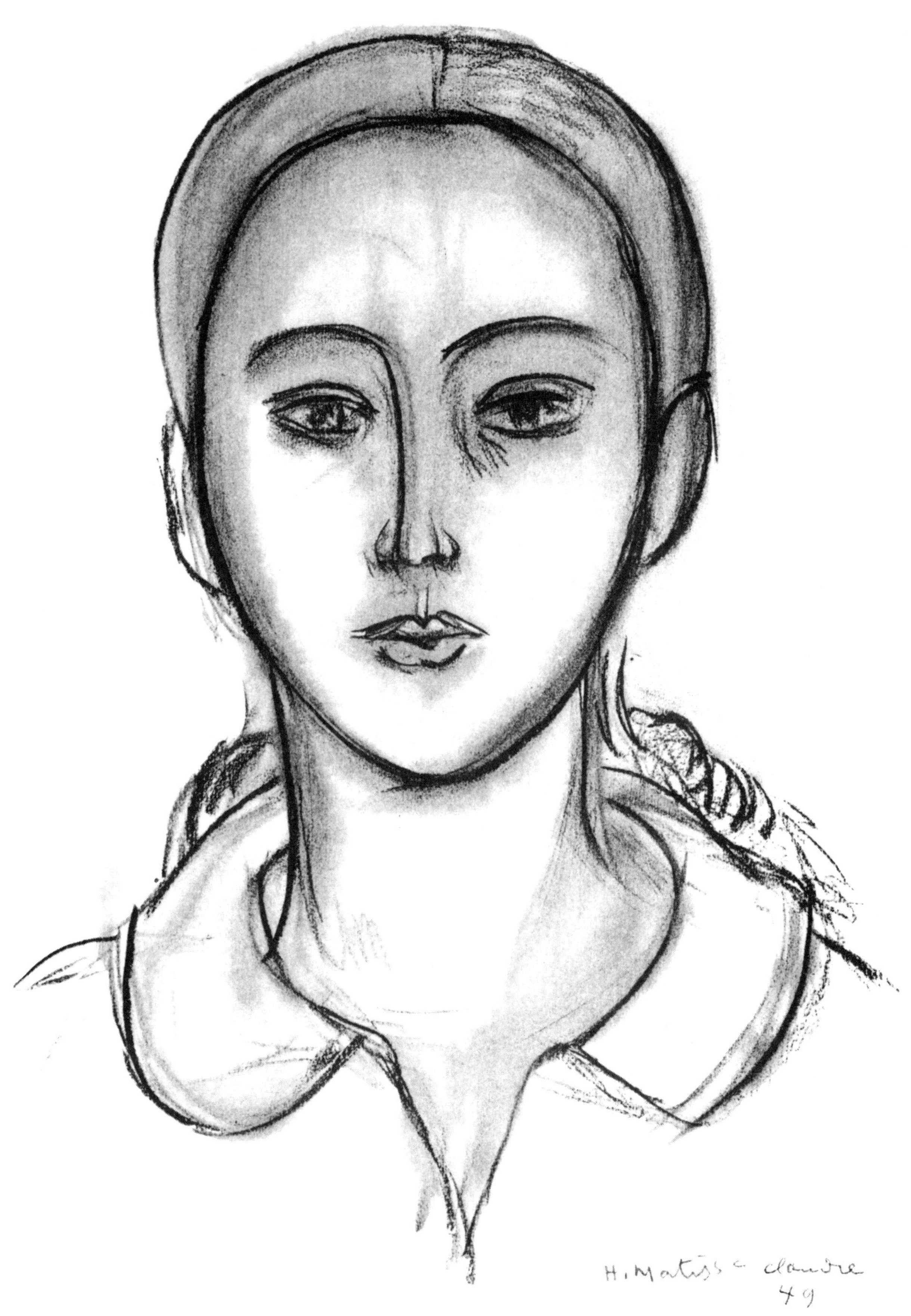

C. P., 1949. Charcoal.

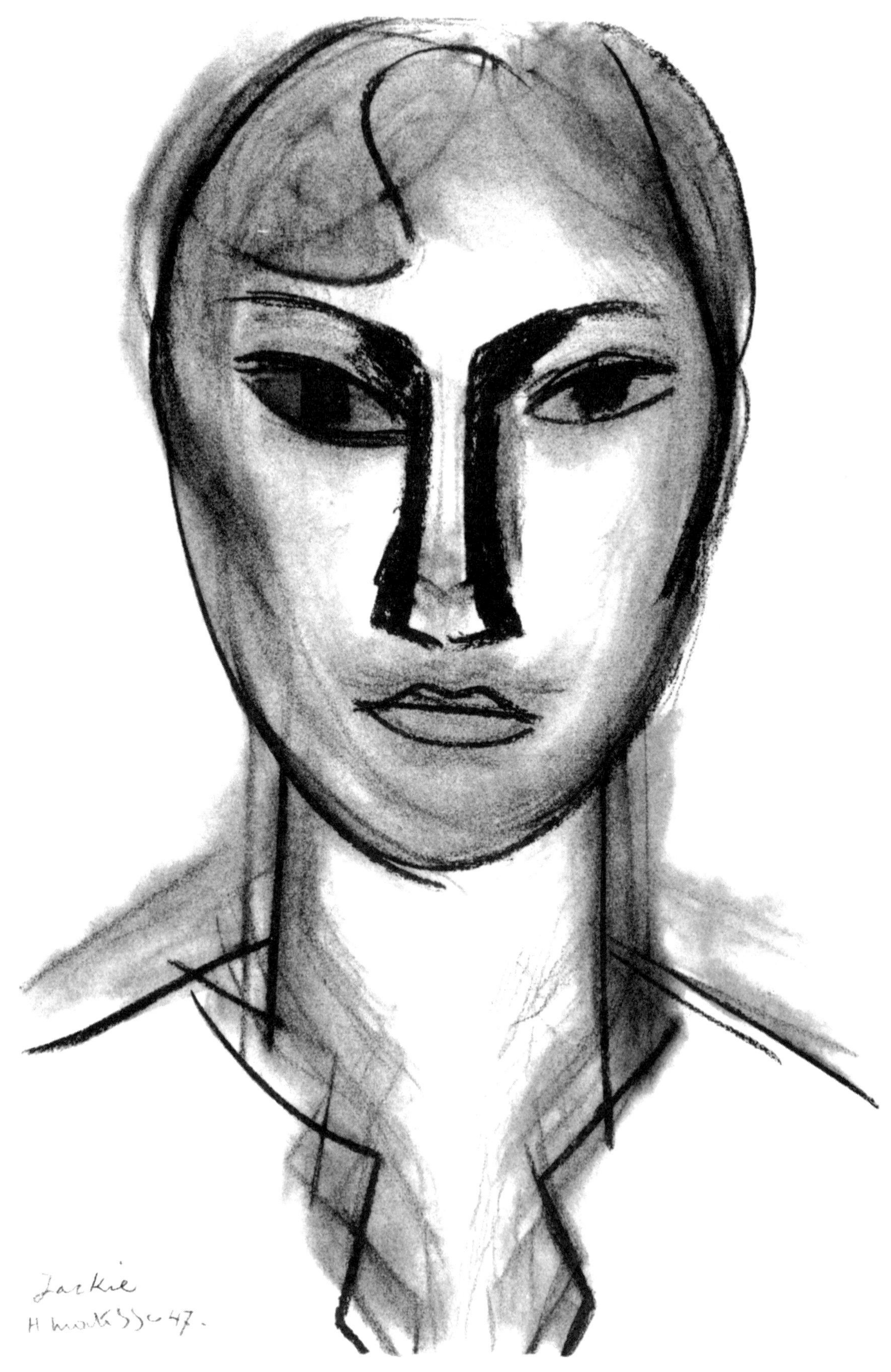

Jacqueline Matisse, 1947. Charcoal.

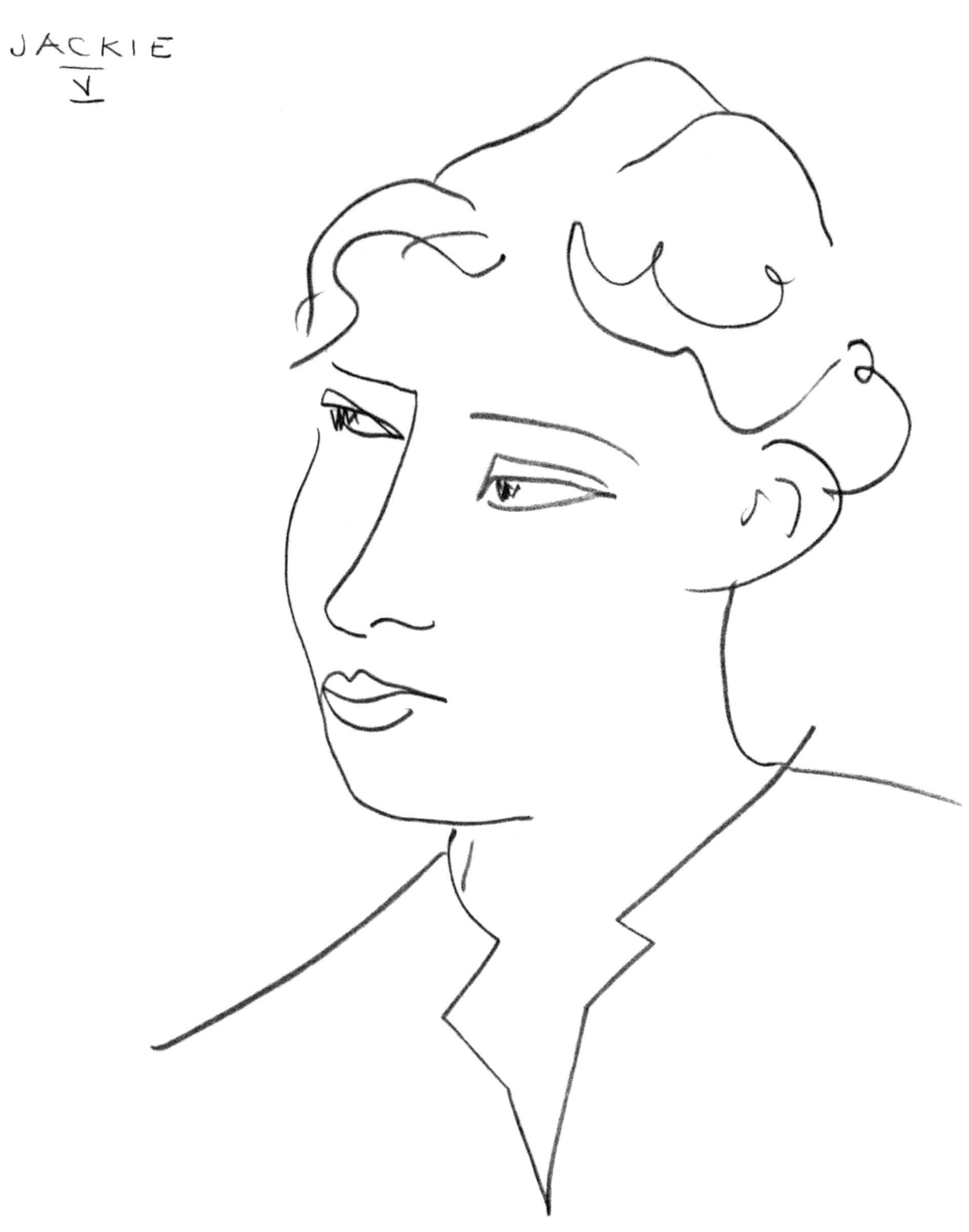

Jacqueline Matisse, 1947. Conté crayon.

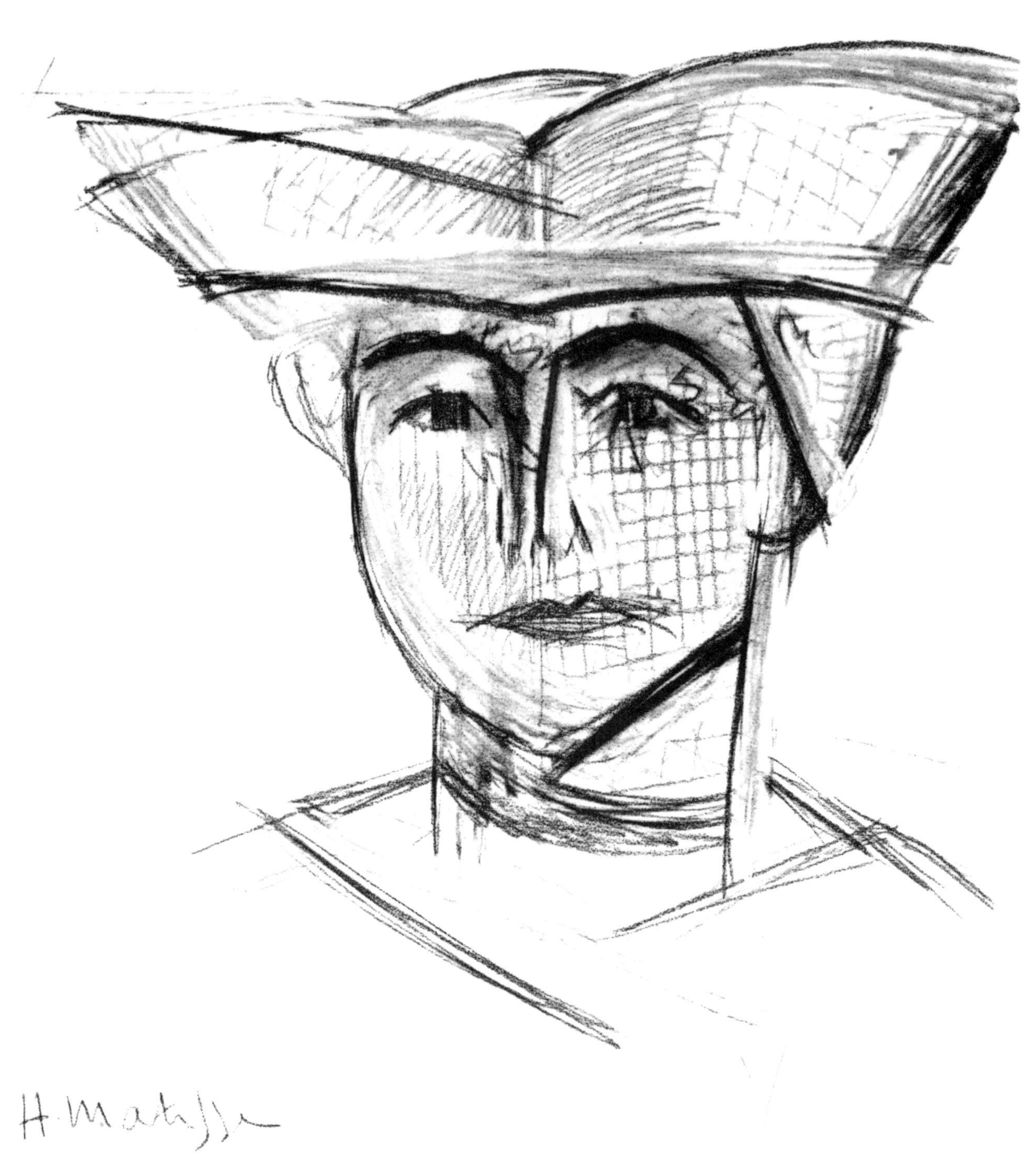

Mme. H. Matisse, 1916. Charcoal, 63 × 48 cm.

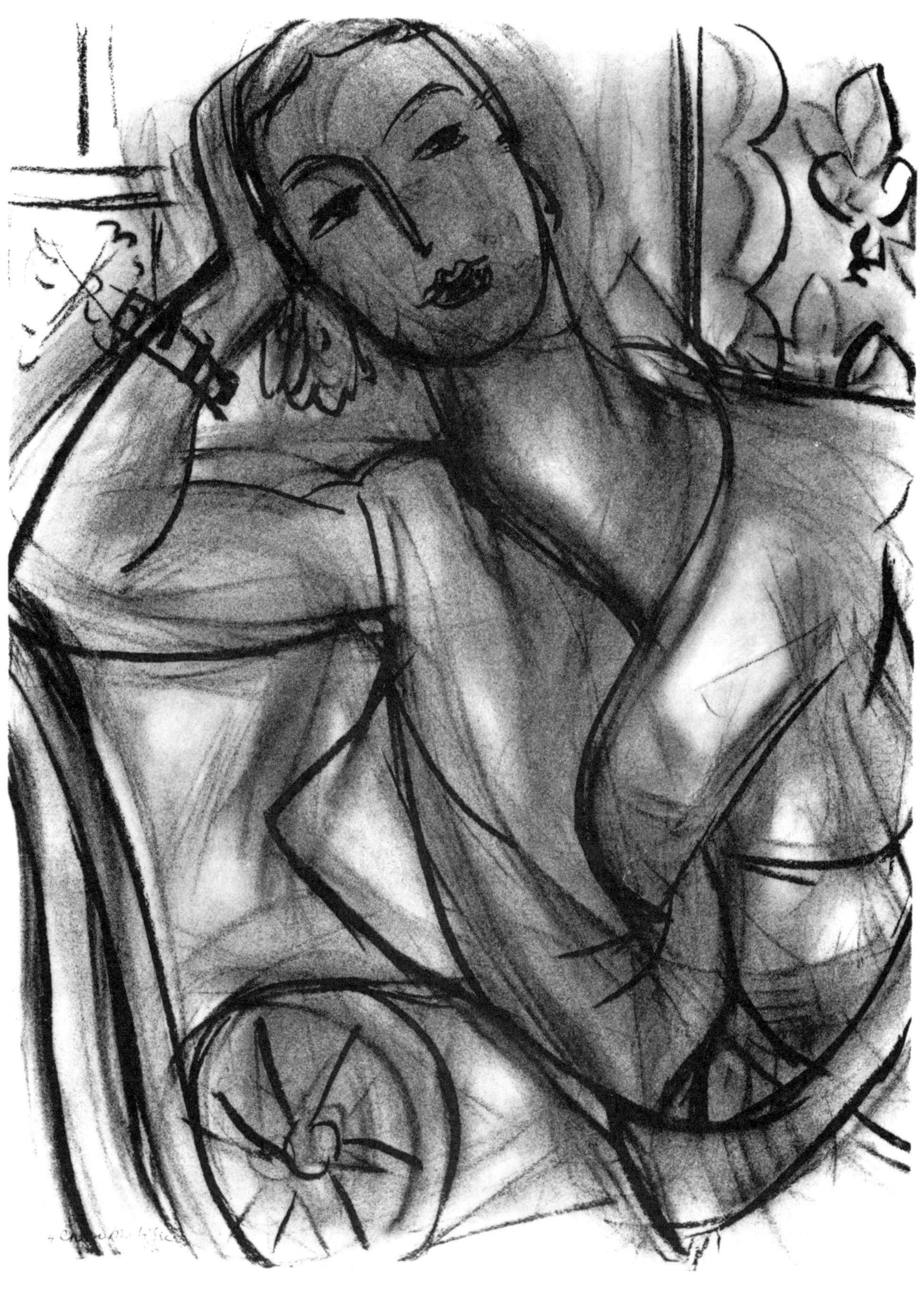

Mary Hutchinson, 1937. Charcoal.

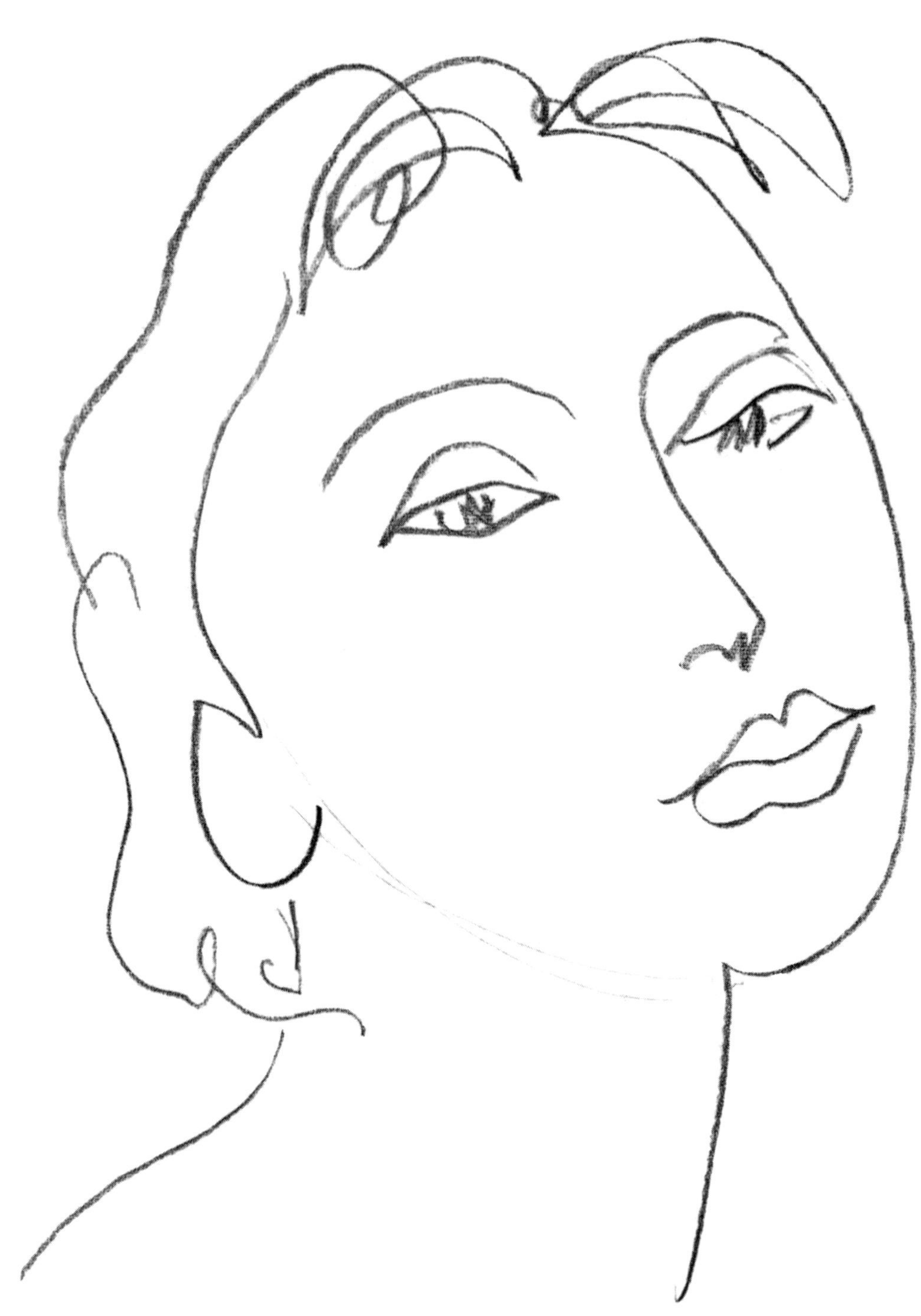

D. A., 1947. Conté crayon, 48 × 31 cm.

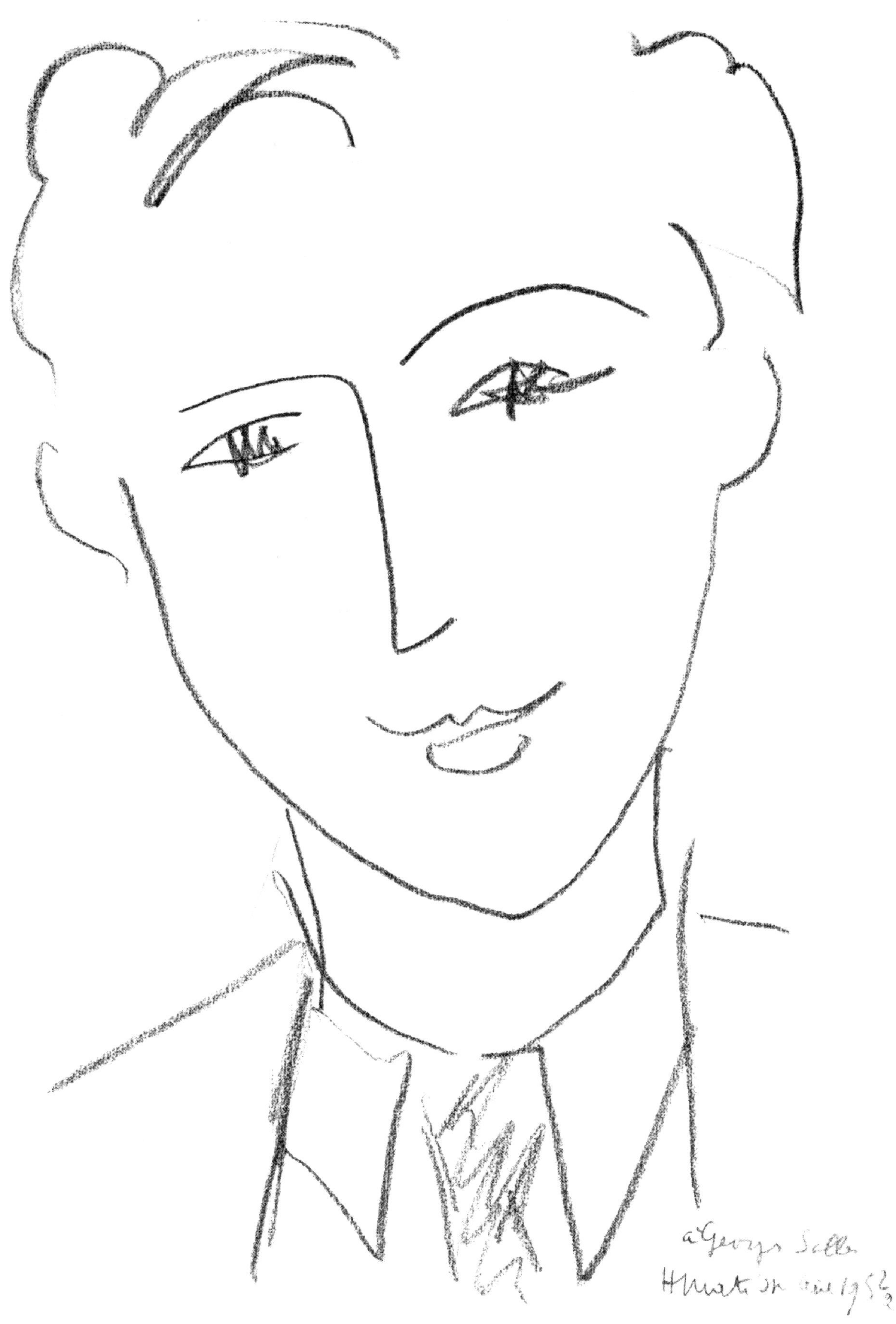

Georges Salles, 1952. Conté crayon, 41 × 31 cm.

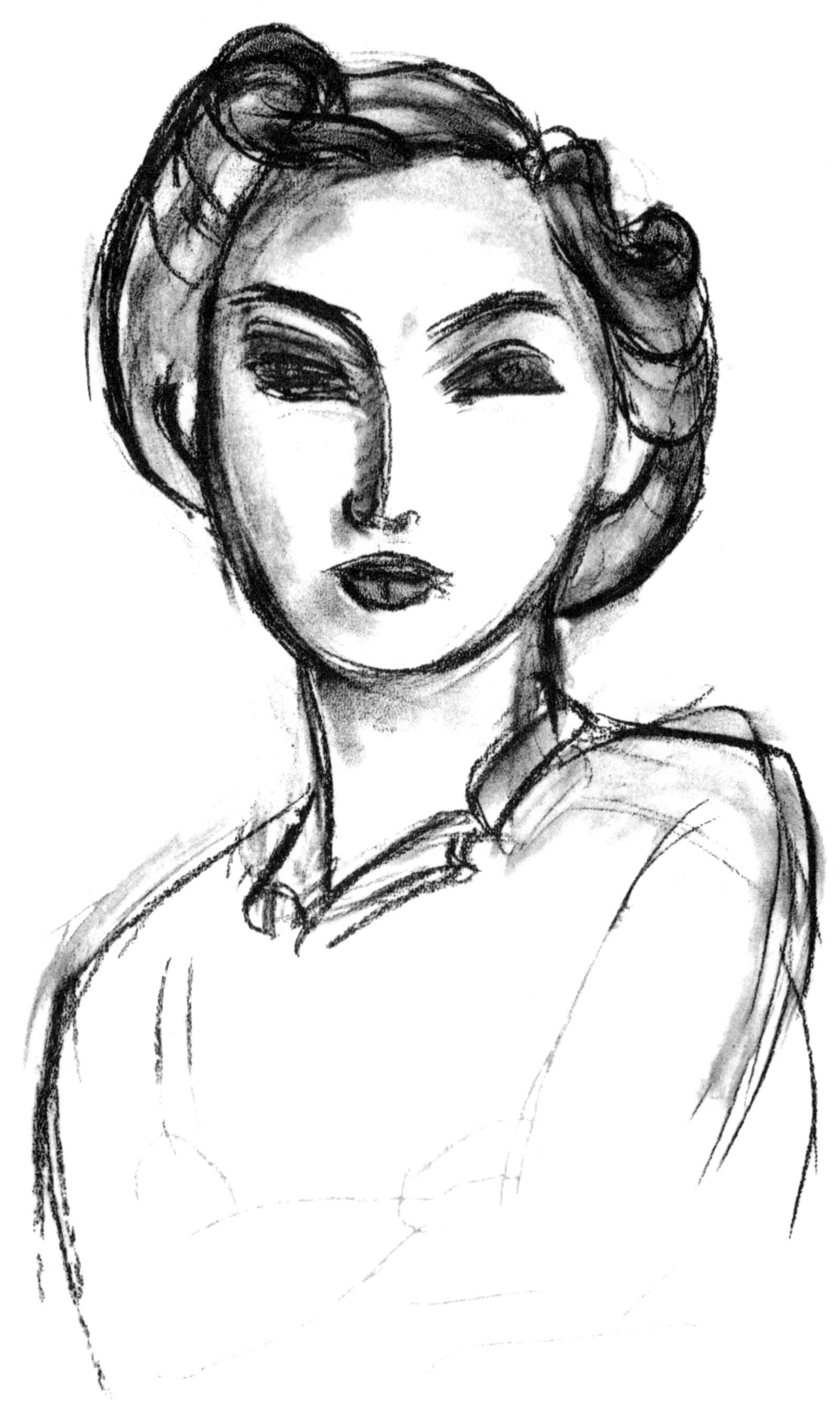

Dorothy Paley, 1937. Charcoal, 66 × 50 cm.

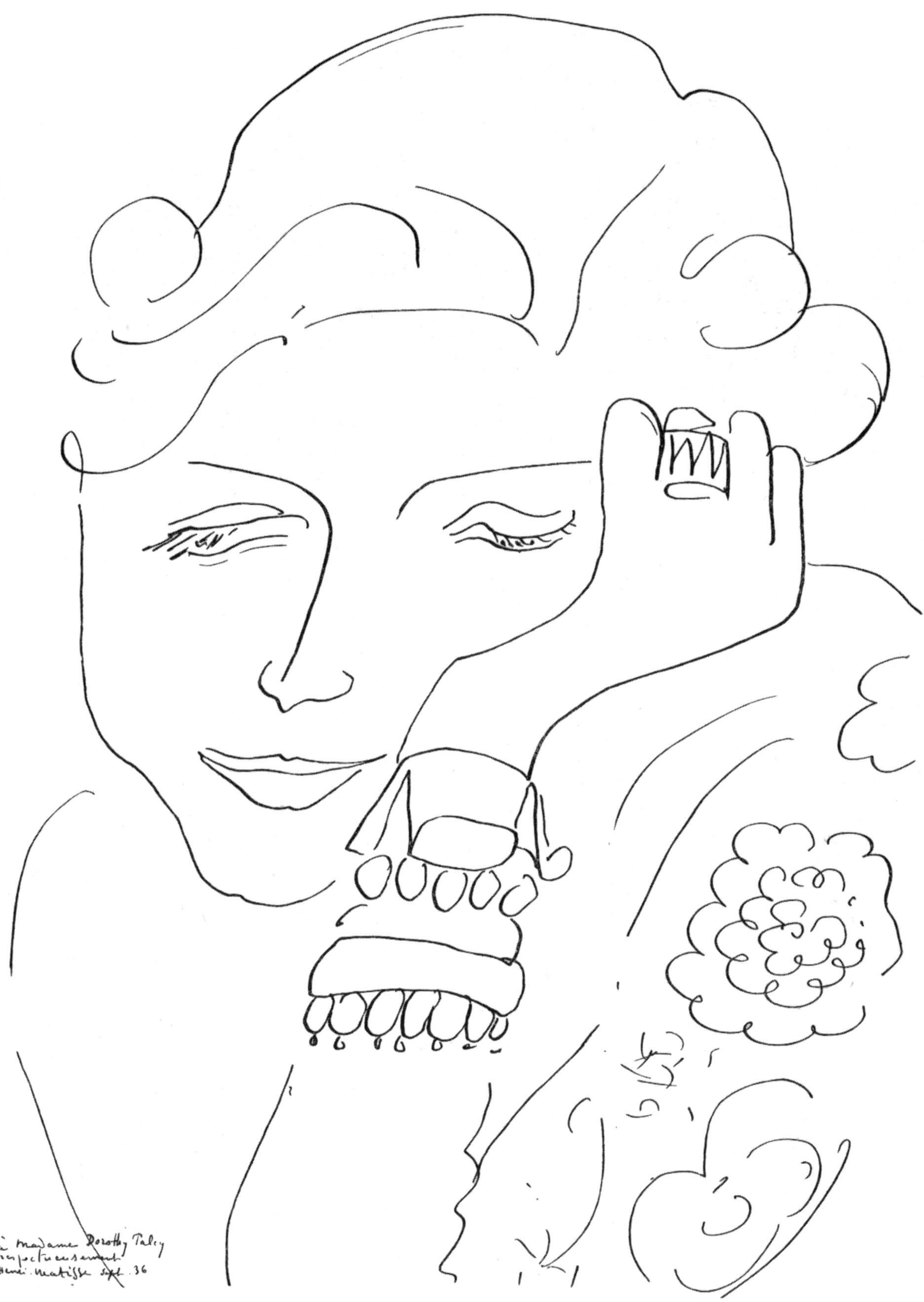

Dorothy Paley, 1936. Pen and india ink.

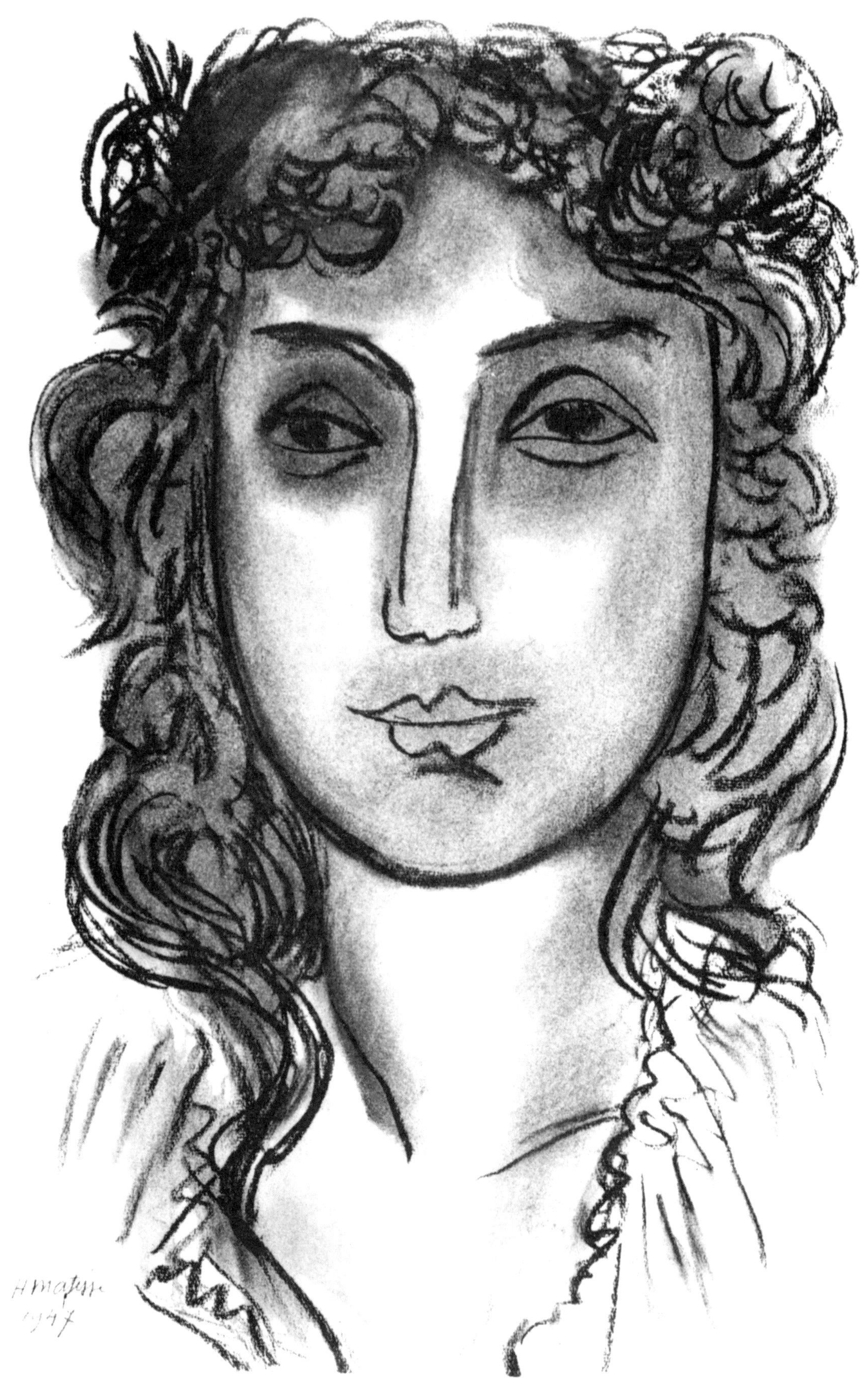

P. C., 1947. Charcoal, 48 × 31 cm.

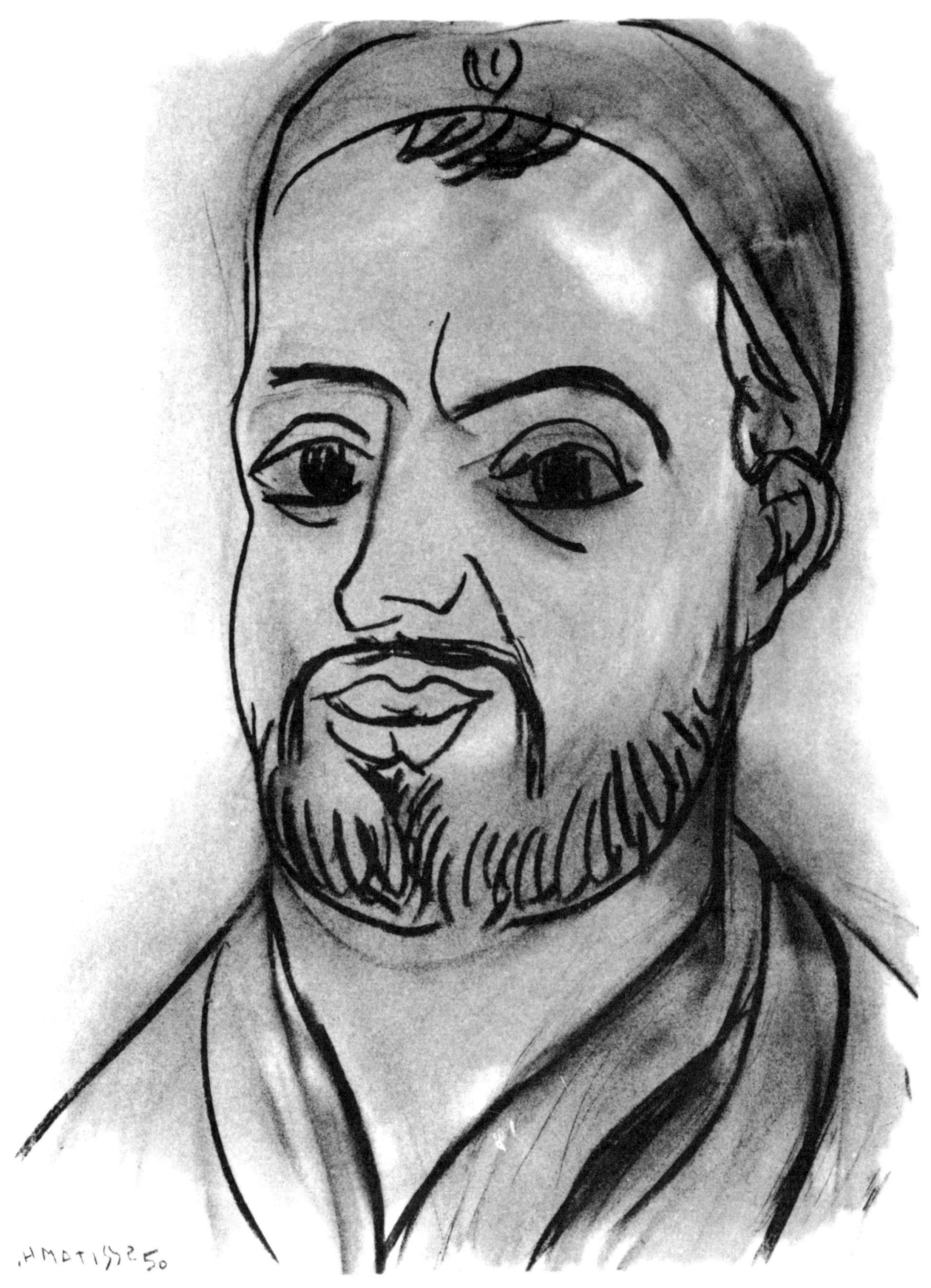

François Rabelais (ca. 1483–1553), 1950. Charcoal, 52 × 40 cm.

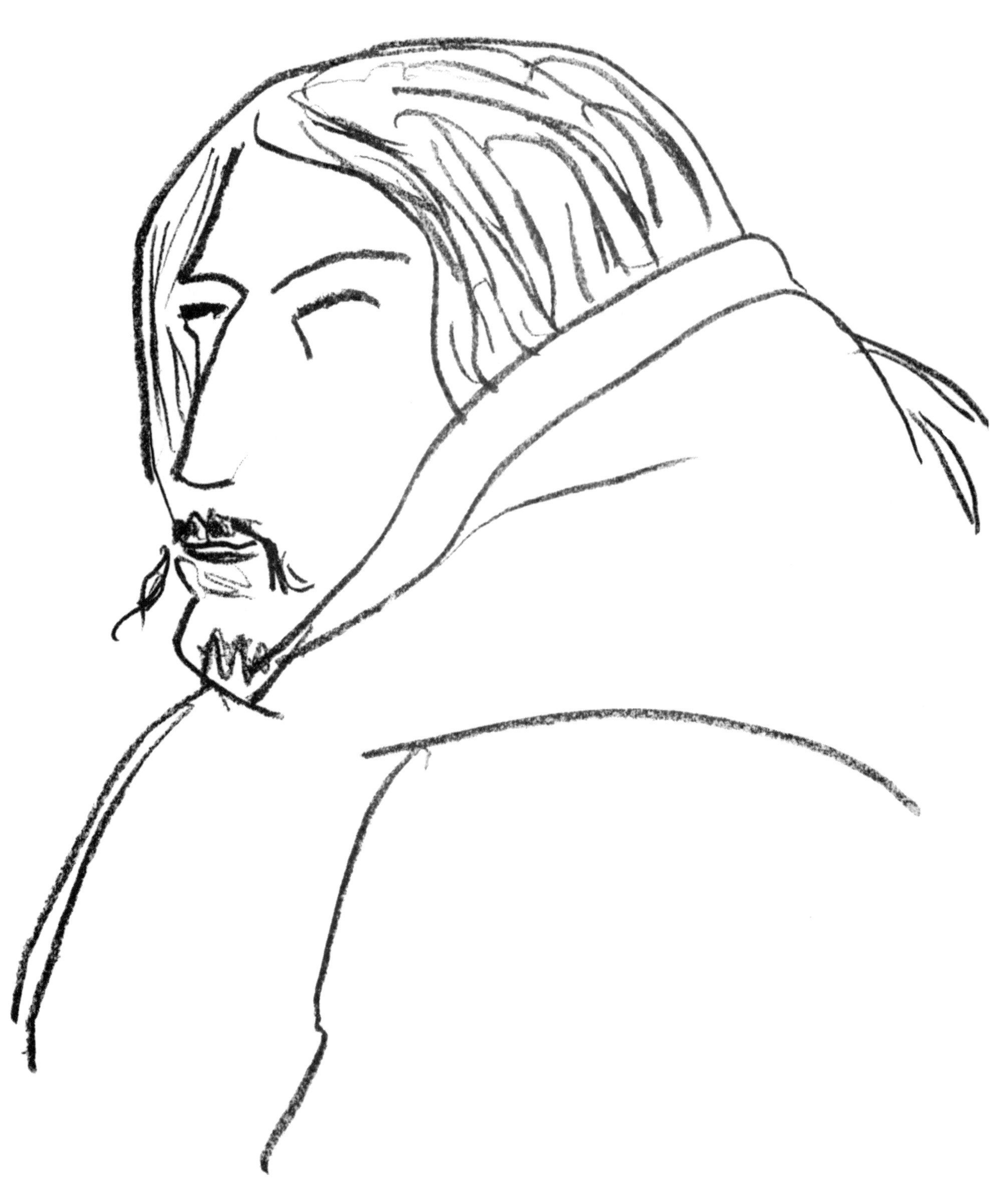

An Eskimo, 1949. Lithograph, 22 × 17 cm.

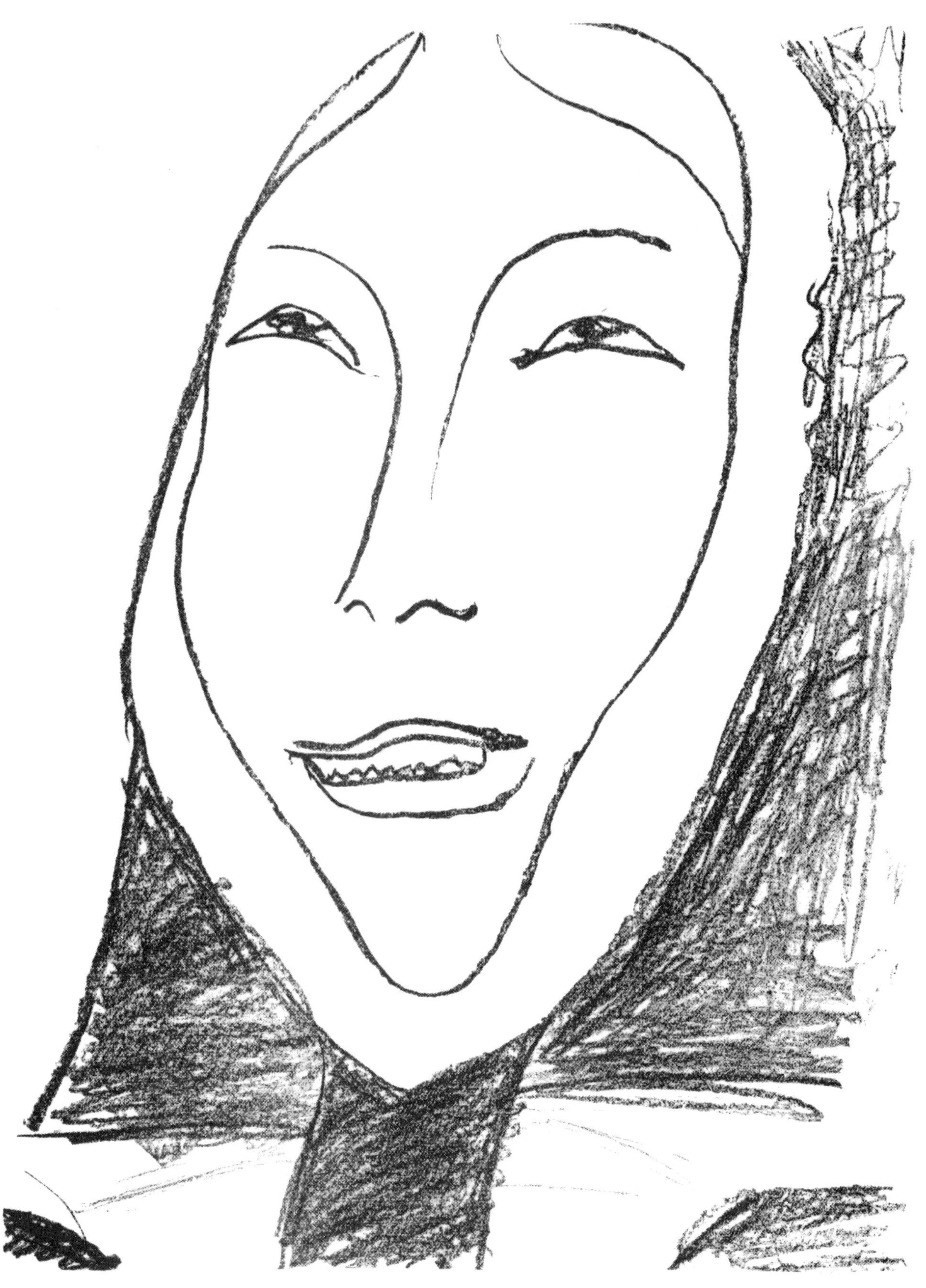

An Eskimo, 1949. Lithograph, 22 × 17 cm.

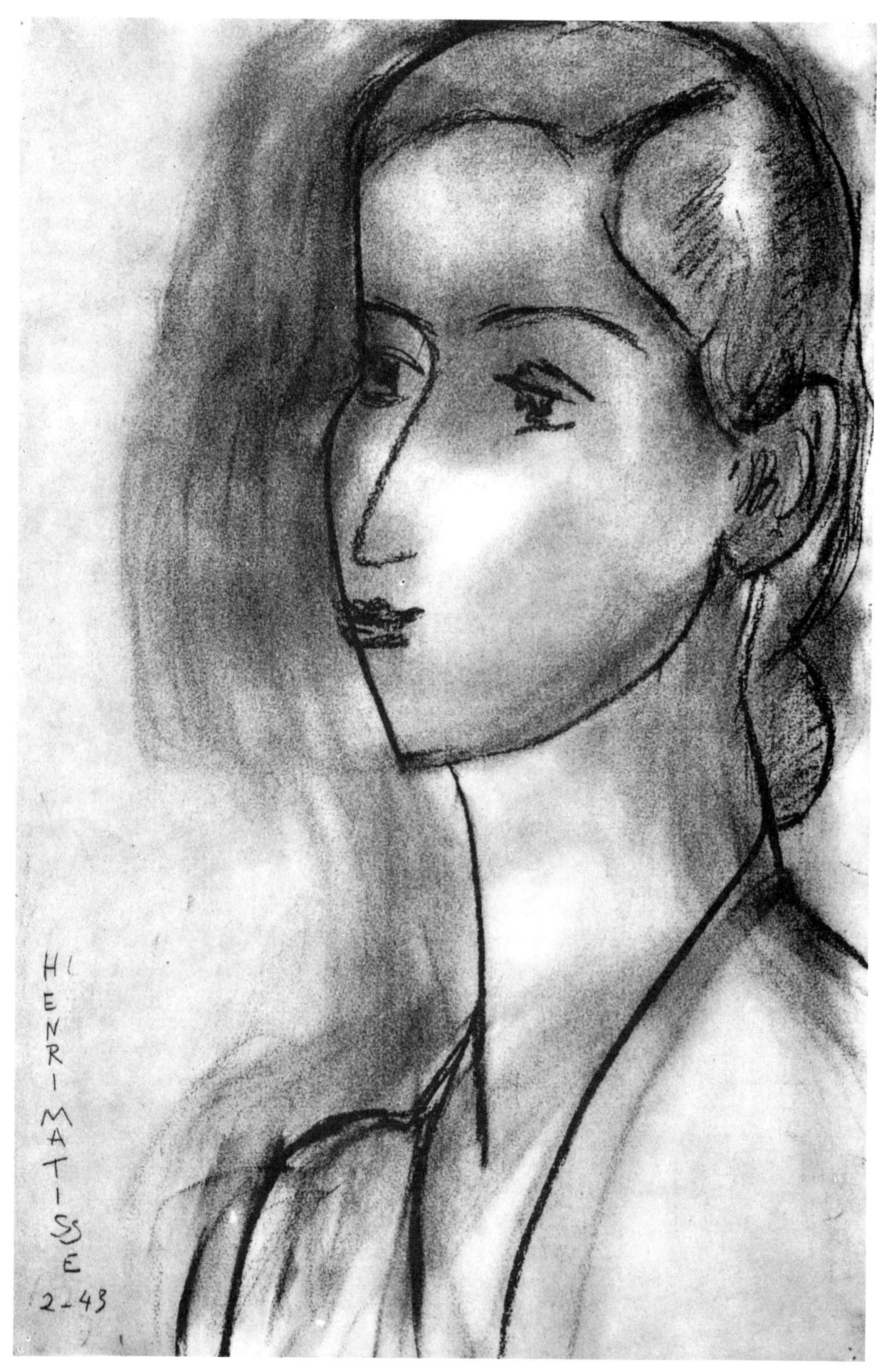

J. Leriche, 1943. Charcoal.

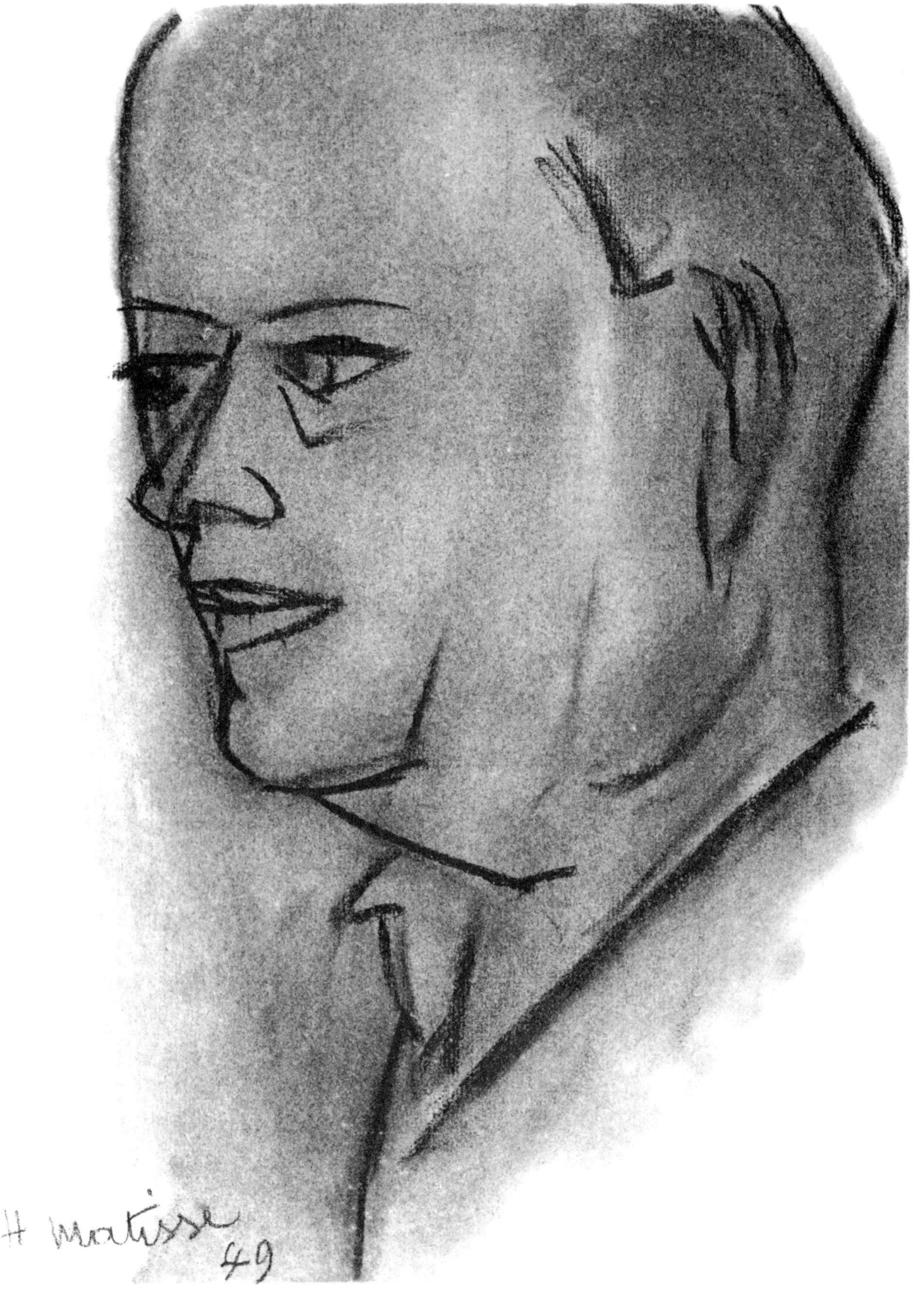

Professor René Leriche, 1949. Charcoal, 31.5 × 24 cm.

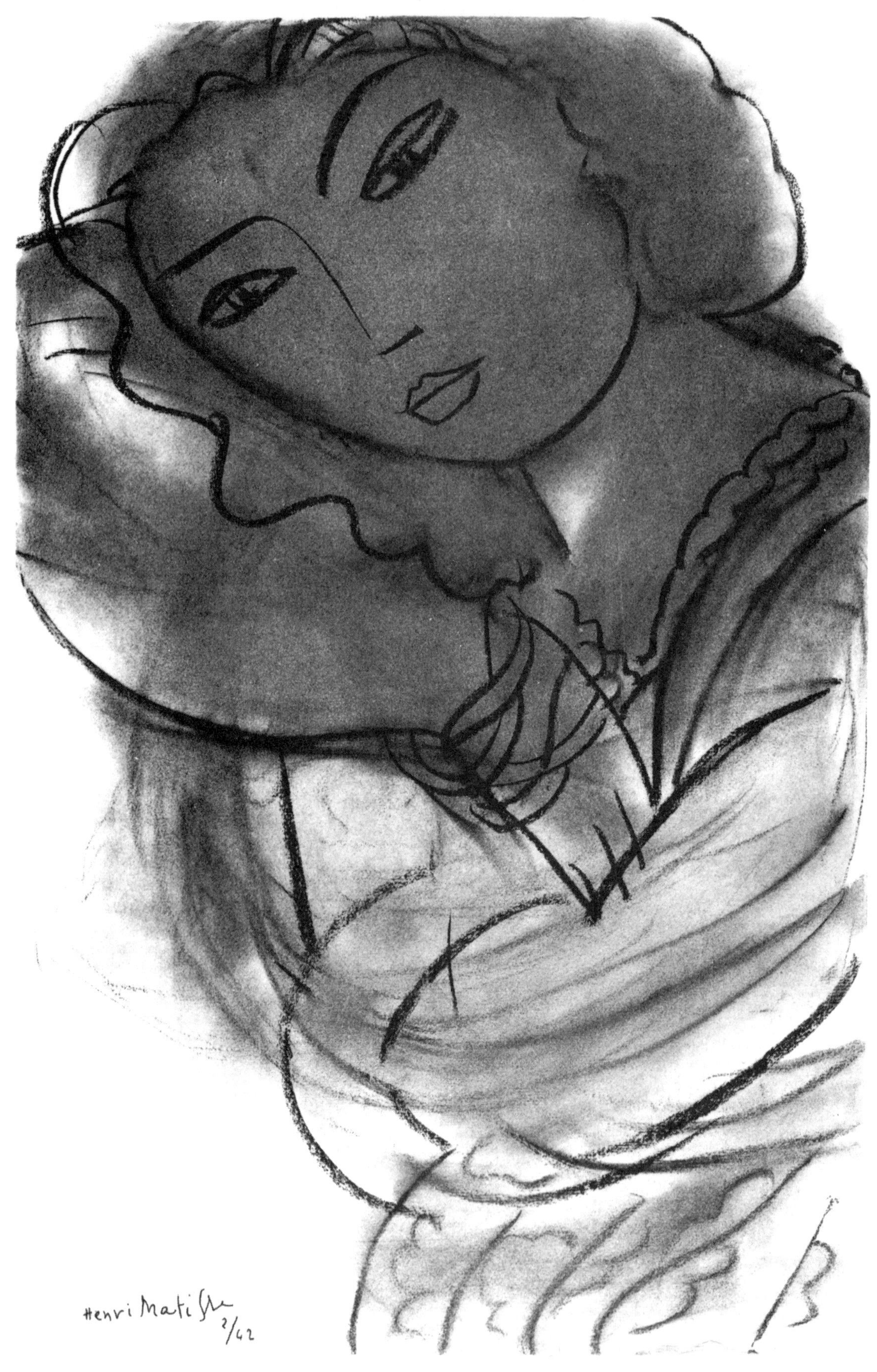

M. A., 1942. Charcoal, 40 × 26 cm.

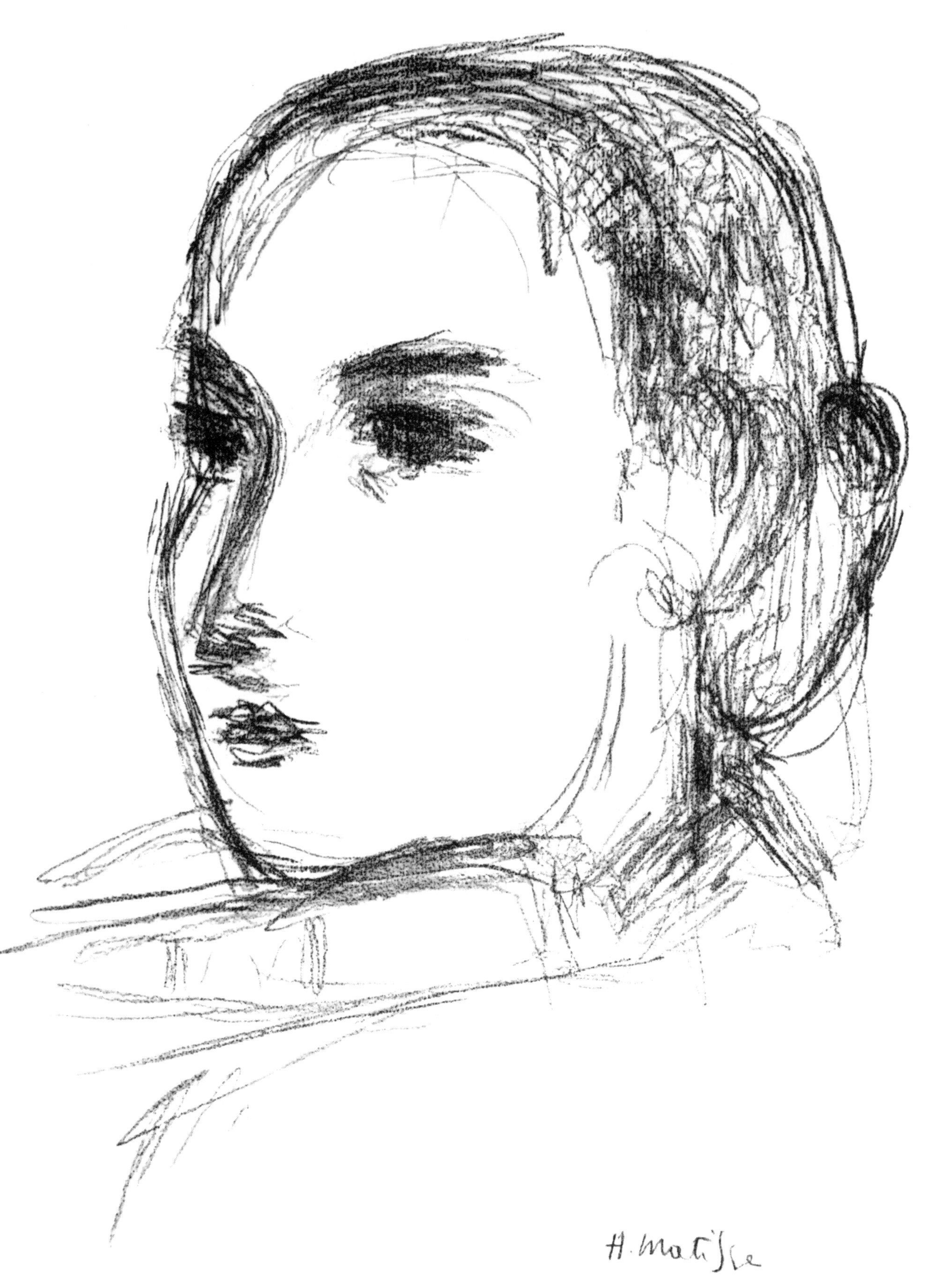

Suzanne Bistesi, 1952. Charcoal, 41 × 31 cm.

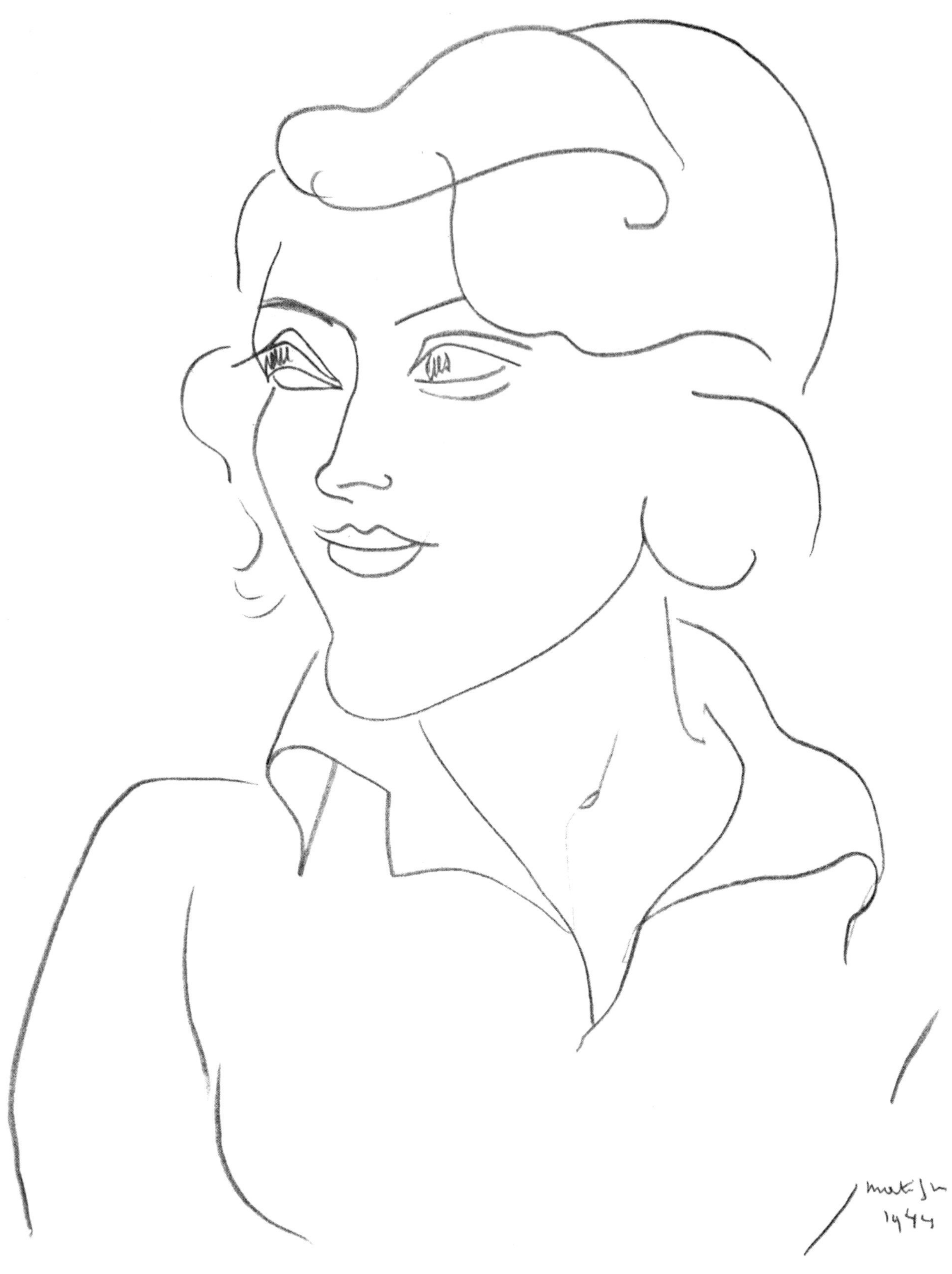

A. Nelck, 1944. Conté crayon, 52 × 40 cm.